What People Wore

EASTERN AMERICAN FAMILY, EARLY 1850S

What PEOPLE WORE

A Visual History of Dress
from Ancient Times to Twentieth-Century America

written and illustrated by

DOUGLAS GORSLINE

New York
THE VIKING PRESS

To

E. P. G.

COPYRIGHT 1951, 1952 BY DOUGLAS GORSLINE

PUBLISHED BY THE VIKING PRESS IN SEPTEMBER 1952

PUBLISHED ON THE SAME DAY IN THE DOMINION OF CANADA
BY THE MACMILLAN COMPANY OF CANADA LIMITED

A few of the drawings in this book appeared in *Harper's* magazine.

LIBRARY OF CONGRESS CATALOG CARD NUMBER: 52-12392

NINTH PRINTING AUGUST 1971

Contents

Titles and numbers in italics refer to illustrations

PART III. AMERICAN COSTUME

Introduction

I have long felt that there was a need for a costume book that would include both clear, accurate drawings and chronologically dated pages. With these requirements in mind, I undertook to compile such a book to help artists, illustrators, designers, writers, and others interested in the appearance of people in earlier times — a book that would give them a workable, visual encyclopedia of historical dress, and which would also contain sufficiently detailed source information to simplify specialized research if that were needed. I hope that I have succeeded not only insofar as my own requirements go, but with regard to the needs of others.

This book opens with a very brief review of the Ancient World. European trends are then traced in greater detail from the medieval period to World War I. Although Americans aped European fashions until recent times, the American way of life brought about variations in clothing, and these I have tried to present more graphically than has heretofore been attempted. Nineteenth-century America produced an entirely native life — that of the frontier. In these regions a real, if short-lived, folk dress developed — one which has never been reported with great detail. In order to survey these widely different trends and to point out distinctions between American and European styles of a given period, I have begun the American section with 1840, when photography became rather usual, and have traced American costume through to 1925 — just yesterday.

My text does little more than trace the general style changes. In a volume which is essentially pictorial, a minimum amount of explanatory material seemed desirable. The serious student of costume is referred to the extensive bibliographies and lists of source material given at the back of the book.

Brief historical chronologies have been added to the text where they seem pertinent — including general background history as well as some of the authors, artists, and scientists of a period. These data, concerned chiefly with Western Europe and England, are only fragmentary, but I hope they will enable the student more easily to relate the costumes to his knowledge of historical events and figures.

In using this book, the reader will easily grasp the chronological arrangement of the material by referring to the Table of Contents, where the periods and areas covered are listed in detail. Since my intention is to provide a historical survey of dress — especially in Europe from the ninth to the twentieth centuries, and in America in the nineteenth and twentieth centuries — such a listing seems more practical than an index under subject headings. I have also presented, in the back of the book, a complete list of sources, identified by page and figure, and bibliographies for the European and American sections.

The question may be asked: Why did I not use photographic illustrations instead of making drawings from source materials of the period? My chief reason is that, in general, reproduction of photographs sacrifices clarity and detail. Furthermore, the original photograph may be cluttered with irrelevant background material that takes up valuable space and at the same time distracts attention from the part in which one is interested. It seemed to me both more practical and more esthetic to make new drawings from the best examples available, carefully and with devotion. In doing these drawings — quite an undertaking, I now realize — I have assumed the responsibility for accuracy, which I sincerely hope I have fulfilled. I have also tried to suggest as skillfully as possible the mannerisms of the times I portray, so that descriptive backgrounds may not be missed too greatly. Where possible, especially in recent times, I have chosen sources more lively and unhackneyed than those usually found. It was not possible to do this for the earlier periods; thus a costume expert will see reproductions from many well-known paintings. However, the source material I have employed for the years following 1840 has not, to my knowledge, been used previously. Much of this has been taken from photographic archives, which provide a great reservoir of new material. I have only skimmed the surface of this valuable store, and suggest that other encyclopedists may well devote more careful attention to it. Few people realize the quantity of existing photographs recording with matchless fidelity the appearance of our ancestors. Photography has been practiced as an art form for one hundred and twenty years, and during the first fifty of those years pictures were perhaps even more realistic than those taken subsequently. There is haunting, nostalgic reality which this medium alone can convey. In compiling a book such as this, which tries to present people as they really appeared and acted, the study of photographs has been of inestimable value.

A criticism of some of the existing costume books is that they tend to overlook the character of the people who wore a given type of dress. I feel that the clothing cannot be considered separately from the people who wore it; therefore I have tried to the best of my ability to portray the human being as well as his dress. People do not change greatly; but the social environment, the pretensions of an age, change, and, changing, have direct effect upon appearance. It is variations such as these that interest me and that I have tried to capture.

The success of such a large undertaking is always dependent upon the generous help of those who have specialized knowledge. Mr. Paul Vanderbilt, of the Library of Congress, gave me much aid and inspired advice in photographic research there. Mr. Beaumont Newhall, Curator of the George Eastman House, Rochester, New York, kindly allowed me to use that museum's very important collection of photographs. Miss Polaire Weissman, Director of the Costume Institute of the Metropolitan Museum, and her staff members, were exceedingly cooperative; the Museum Library and its Print Collection always provided hospitable refuge for this harried researcher. The New York Historical Society, through its Curator of Prints, Mr. Carlson, proved a rich field for research. I wish also to thank Miss Grace Mayer, Curator of Prints and Photographs of the Museum of the City of New York, for her aid with the important Byron collection. The New York Public Library is a mine of informative Americana, and I am especially grateful to Mr. Sylvester Vigilante, of the American History Room, who gave me a great deal of help on sources.

For help in preparing the material on the American cowboy, I wish to thank Mr. Struthers Burt of Jackson Hole, Wyoming; the Levi Strauss Company of San Francisco; Mr. Ross Santee of Arden, Delaware; and Mr. Eugene D. Brown of Scottsville, New York. I have also used valuable information from Philip Ashton Rollins' authoritative book, *The Cowboy*.

D. G.

Part I
COSTUME OF THE ANCIENT WORLD

GREEK CHARIOTEER

Egypt and the Near East

SINCE the main concern of this book is with Western European clothing from the medieval period to the twentieth century, I have not illustrated the costume of the ancient world in any detail. However, it seems worth while to show the basic dress which early peoples developed. All clothing probably originated with the loin-cloth; the next development was the tunic.

The ancient world was one in which the rulers, nobles, priestly classes, and warriors maintained themselves in absolute power over the great masses of people. It was thus a society in which one general style of clothing could survive for thousands of years. What changes occurred were precipitated by periods of power and wealth or by reactions against display, but these changes took place within the rather limited confines of one type of style.

The ancient world's pattern of strict social stratification persisted in India and China until the twentieth century. As the civilizations of the Western world developed, however, there was increasing insistence on class emancipation or individualism, reflected in dress as well as in other cultural patterns. Thus there is a marked costume differentiation between the East's quasi-permanent styles and the West's changeableness: to the northwest of the Mediterranean, individualism; to the east and southeast, submergence of the person into the mass.

Since the climate of Egypt was very warm, nakedness was common; and modesty, in our present cultural sense of the word, did not exist. The basic fabric was linen of various grades, according to the wearer's station. Garments were usually white.

Loincloths were worn by all classes of men; clothing of the poorer classes was made of coarser materials. Kings' garments were often decorated with gold. With the passage of time the loincloth developed into a tight-fitting skirt called the kalasiris, fastened high up under the arms. Later this became two skirts, the outer one perhaps of filmy material; and still later the outer skirt was discarded.

Women wore tight-fitting sheaths from breasts to ankle, which were attached at the shoulders by straps. Working women might wear a short kalasiris which left the breasts bare. Servants were usually naked. From the Fifth to the Eighteenth Dynasty (c. 2750-1580 B.C.) both men and women shaved their heads and wore wigs — often brightly colored — the women's almost invariably longer, fuller, and more elaborately stylized than men's.

The Asiatic costume was more complex than the Egyptian of a comparable period; thus as far back as the nineteenth or twentieth century B.C. there are representations of Semites wearing close-fitting tunics and cloaks which are often richly patterned or ornamented with fringe or tassels. Joseph's "coat of many colors" probably dated from this era.

In Egypt after the Eighteenth Dynasty (c. 1580-1350 B.C.) more attention was paid to appearance, and an age of luxury overshadowed the simplicity that had prevailed earlier. At this time flowing sleeves, pleated skirts, and the sheer cape were introduced, as well as lavish jewelry and ornaments that made use of gold, semiprecious stones, and glass. Cloth was woven and embroidered in geometric patterns, and strong primary colors were commonly used.

From the Eighteenth to the Twentieth Dynasty (c. 1580-1200 B.C.) the Syrian influence markedly altered Egyptian styles: at this time silky-coated sheep were introduced; and with sheep came woolen garments. Egypt was conquered in 664 B.C. by the Assyrians, and its power, which had already begun to decline, grew even less. At about the Twenty-fifth Dynasty (712-663 B.C.) the earlier simplicity of costume returned. Later the successive pre-eminence of Persia, of Greece, of Rome, overshadowed the culture of Egypt even before its conquest by the Moslems in 640 A.D.

4

Draped shawl

Royal attendant

Slave girl

Nineteenth Dynasty

Royal costume

Middle Empire

Egyptian dignitaries and peasants

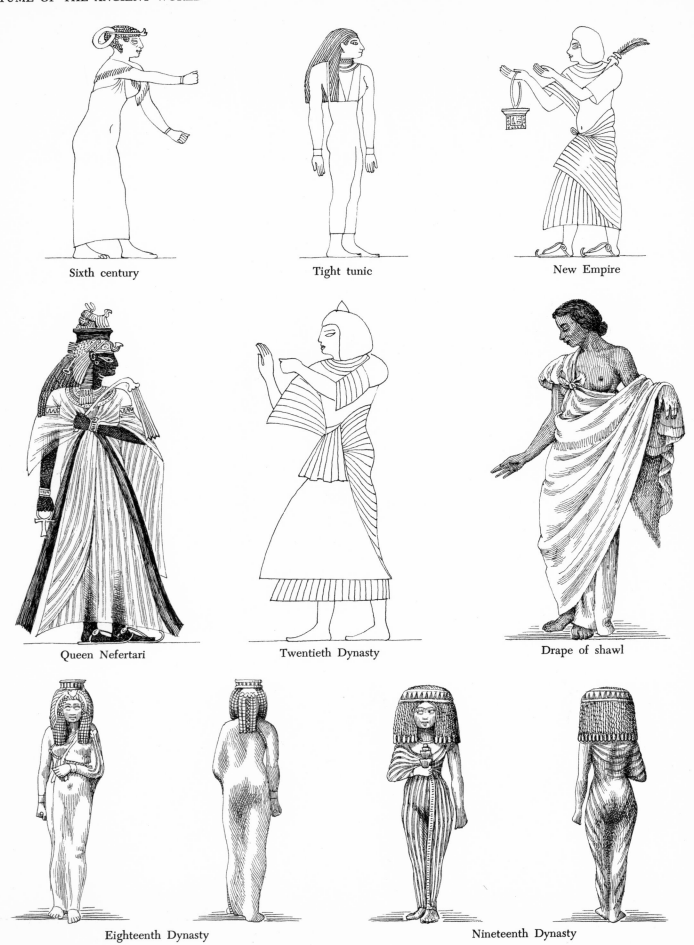

Sixth century

Tight tunic

New Empire

Queen Nefertari

Twentieth Dynasty

Drape of shawl

Eighteenth Dynasty

Nineteenth Dynasty

Religious and secular headdresses

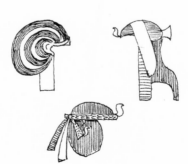

Loincloth

Sandals

Styles in Egyptian headdress

Persian merchant

Hebraic religious

Persian noble

Assyrian commoner

Assyrian noble

Assyrian deity

Cretan lady

Cretan soldier

Cretan citizen

Cretan lady

Greece and Rome

THE HIGHLY elaborate culture of the Cretans (*c.* 3400-1000 B.C.), a precursor of the Greek, was reflected in their beautifully cut, fitted, and often patterned clothing. Men wore a loincloth under an apron, a tight girdle at the waist, and high boots of ornamented leather. Helmets were decorated and crested. Men's hair, like women's, was long, often knotted at the nape of the neck. The upper torsos of women were originally bared; later the fashion of tight waist bindings, a series of aprons which resembled long skirts, and the exposure of the breasts in a calculated bodice frame was adopted. Capes had high stand-up collars. Head coverings were complicated horned, conical, or turban arrangements worn over long and often snakelike hair dressings. Cretan clothing is of special interest to us, since it was startlingly similar to later Western styles, yet occurred nowhere else in the ancient world.

In Greek and Roman costume the influence of pagan ethics and a bland climate is still apparent; thus there was considerable nakedness. Clothes were strikingly loose and free; perhaps at no other time in history have such practical and very graceful garments been popular. Greece was to the later Rome as Paris was to eighteenth- and nineteenth-century Europe — the source of art and style.

The one indispensable garment of early Greece was the chiton, worn by both men and women. This was a large rectangular piece of dyed and often embroidered wool draped over the body so as to cover the left arm; the right arm was left free. Back and front were then fastened at the shoulders with brooches, or fibulae. The borders of the cloth were frequently decorated with geometrical designs. The chiton was either knee-length or long; both profession and degree of activity apparently dictated the amount of leg room allowed the wearer. A later variant of this basic garment was fuller and softer, often pleated and caught at the waist by a girdle. The appearance of sleeves was developed by an orderly placing of small fibulae across the shoulders and down the arms.

Another rectangular woolen garment, the himation, was colored and sometimes embroidered. It was worn by women over their linen chitons; men often wore it as their sole garment. A lighter woolen overgarment, the chlamys, was a short oblong mantle fastened at the right shoulder. It was worn, usually over a short chiton, by horsemen and later by young men of all classes.

In Greece, and later in Rome, these styles reflected the habits of a leisure class; the clothing of working people was more practical. To display wealth, very elaborate and cunningly worked jewelry was popular: earrings, bracelets, necklaces, brooches, rings, and fibulae made chiefly of metal and sometimes of semiprecious stones.

Warriors were armed with breastplates of leather, metal-studded leather, or metal plates sewn on cloth. Crested helmets of leather or bronze varied in size and shape; some covered the entire face. A round iron shield and iron sword were prerogatives only of the leaders; common soldiers carried a bronze or iron spear.

In Rome the tunica was the common article of clothing. The toga, a long, sweeping, semicircular drape, usually white, was worn on important occasions. An embroidered purple toga over a gold-embroidered tunica was affected by magistrates and judges, and Julius Caesar adopted these as his daily costume.

Later, the women's toga was replaced by the palla, which was essentially the Greek himation. The pallium, also similar to the himation, was worn by men over the toga. Both garments were thrown over the head as a hood, but women also invariably wore an additional head covering.

During the Roman imperial age, fashion became a field of heated competition. Lightweight silk undergarments, scarfs, soft furs, and other rare and costly materials, usually richly dyed, were worn, though garments were not as extravagant and magnificent as they became, for instance, in medieval Europe.

Chiton

Design of chiton

Chiton

Himation

Chiton

Chiton

Chlamys

Design of chlamys

Chiton

Double-girdled chiton

Bacchante

Dancer

Upper-class lady

Doric peplos

Man wearing chlamys

Lady wearing chiton with himation

Soldier

Orator

Peasant

Soldier

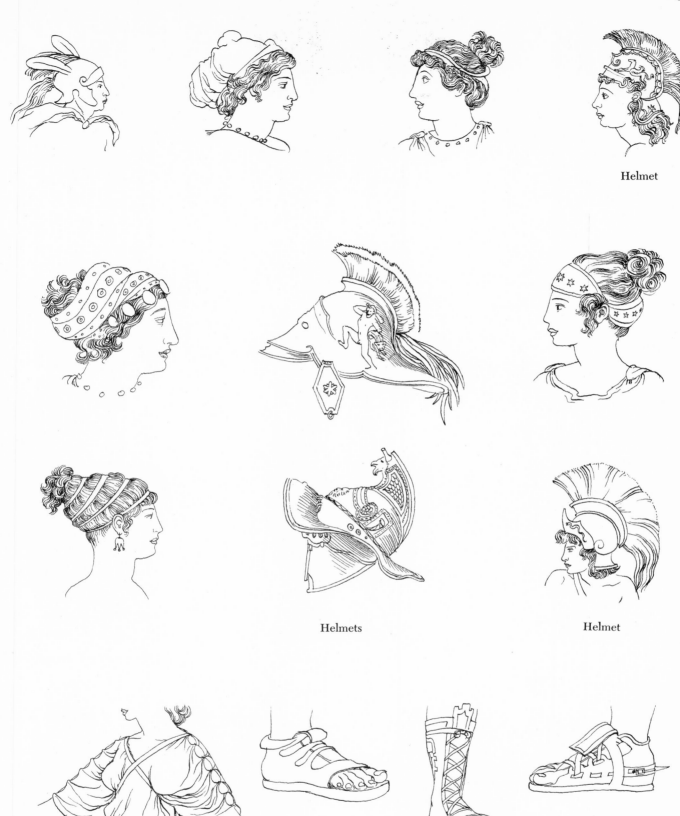

Helmet

Helmets

Helmet

Chiton binding

Grecian footwear

Roman lady

Gladiator

Roman lady

Priestly toga

Roman in overtoga

Roman lady with palla

Roman centurion

Roman wearing palla

Young Roman

Soldier

14

Roman headdress

Byzantine lady

Byzantine commoners

Byzantine nobles

Two Byzantine gentlemen

Byzantine religious

Part II
EUROPEAN COSTUME

DONOR OF "THE HOLY LAMB," AFTER VAN EYCK

The Medieval Period

WHEN the Romans arrived in England they found men and women fully clothed and well protected against the cold climate. Men wore sleeved, short-skirted coats and loose trousers, with cloaks and simple hats for colder weather. They also had tightly fitting leather garments and furs. Women's ankle-length gowns were covered by an outer short tunic. These people were dyers as well as weavers. They wore colored garments and massive gold armbands, rings, brooches, and pins. Men had no armor, but their tightly woven felt coverings were almost swordproof.

Across the Channel pre-Norman dress was also simple. Men wore short, loose, sleeveless smocks or tunics caught at the waist with leather thongs; Gallic breeches, tied around the waist; and as hose, either fabric or an extension of the breeches cross-gartered below the knee. A calf-length mantle, fastened at the shoulder, usually covered the head, but hats and caps were rare. Ankle-height shoes had pointed tabs in front and behind. Nobles' tunics and shoes were embroidered with silk or yarn. After the time of Charlemagne (*d.* 814) the men wore their hair short. Women's long gowns covered their feet; the sleeves were loose and sometimes extended as low as the knee. Over this garment a shorter tunic was worn. Mantles were either long or short; sometimes they were hooded, and the point of the hood could be wrapped around the chin. Fine gloves and handkerchiefs were used.

In battle a ruler would be completely armored, and even the common soldier had metal armlets, helmet, leg protection, and shield.

When the Normans invaded Britain they adopted some fashions, such as that of wearing long hair and beards, which they carried back to the Continent; but in general Norman dress was taken over by the Britons. With William II (reigned 1087-1100) there was an increase in luxuriousness of clothing. Long cloaks and trailing gowns with sleeves falling far below the level of the hands were adopted, and boots and shoes became exaggeratedly sharp-pointed. Both men and women had long and flowing hair; men's beards gradually became less common.

The period of the Crusades acquainted Europeans for the first time with the East, and it is not surprising that many Oriental influences are noted at this time. In the twelfth century men wore not only long, loose-skirted outer and under tunics with tightly laced, fitted bodices, but also undershirts of linen to which the long hose were attached. A woman's tunic was similar but longer; under this was a linen undergarment, the chemise. By the end of this century an ample fur-lined overgarment, the pelisson, had been adopted by men and women. Hoods were much in use, lengthened at the back to a long point, the liripipe.

During the thirteenth century a comparatively simple cloak became the dominant dress form. Among the upper classes rich furs, silk, or cloth of gold served as linings. Under the cloak was a garment best described as a simple gown; its sleeves were often wide, cut short to show the narrower and longer sleeves of an undergarment. This same basic gown was also worn by working people, but in their case it was cut off at the knees to permit manual labor. Hoods or tight caps tied under the chin were commonly worn by men and women; women also often draped the hair with a piece of fabric that fell to the shoulders.

The basic dress remained rectangular until the late fourteenth and the fifteenth centuries, when society was more sophisticated and complex. Clothing gradually abandoned simple lines and assumed the fantastic richness and elaborateness associated with the later medieval period.

Men's gowns became shorter but still covered the knees. A tailored doublet was developed, and in the second half of the fourteenth century the cote-hardie was imported from Germany. This was a low-necked, laced or buttoned outer garment. It grew shorter and by the middle of the fifteenth century was little more than frock-coat length. The houppelande then became the fashion; this was a long, loose tunic, usually belted, with fitted shoulders, high collar, and flowing sleeves. As materials and workmanship improved, hose became longer and the doublet correspondingly shorter. Sleeves and hem lines were frequently "slittered" or jagged, which gave to clothing much of its opulent, fantastic character. Men's and women's hair was often garlanded with jeweled cloth, and there was great variety in hats, caps, and hoods. Buttons were becoming popular and might adorn a garment or sleeve from top to bottom, quite apart from function.

Women of rank wore loose, trailing gowns, but they also borrowed the men's styles of cote-hardie and houppelande. The feminine modification of the latter had a short-waisted bodice and a belted, gored skirt which often trailed behind. As illustrated here, women's clothing was frequently decorated with heraldric motifs, in the manner of men's armorial bearings.

At the beginning of the fifteenth century man's usual garment was a loose, pleated tunic either lined or edged with fur. Long and baggy sleeves, drawn in tightly at the wrists, were often buttoned. Underneath was another shorter tunic or doublet with close-fitting sleeves fastened at the wrists. A cloak and hood or a hooded cloak was worn over all. A loose girdle belted the waist; suspended from it was the anlace or baselard — the tapering short sword or dagger of the period. Shoes were still exaggeratedly pointed. Many kinds of hats and caps were worn, most of them derivatives of the hood and liripipe of the preceding century. One of the more bizarre styles consisted of a circular roll of cloth bound about the brow and descending on both sides in folds cascading to the shoulder or even to the waist. Everything contributed to an appearance of casual magnificence at once lordly and elegant. As the century drew to a close, the points of shoes became less noticeable and finally disappeared, while the soles broadened and gradually became stubby during the reign of Henry VIII. The dangles from the girdle became tokens: first a purse, later even beads. By the end of the century hose reached to the waistline and the codpiece, introduced earlier in the century, was increasingly evident.

Women adopted men's furred tunics, but their gowns were longer. The gown had a skin-tight bodice, was girdled high under the breasts, and then fell loosely to the ground in wide folds. Sleeves either buttoned tightly or were prolonged as tippets extending far below the hands. A long and plain cloak fastened at the breast with a cord. Religious practices influenced the covering of the hair: cauls were drawn up and around the head into shapes such as hearts or horns; in some, fantastic wired arrangements caused the cambric veiling or wimple to float out behind like a butterfly. By the latter part of the century, however, clothing had become more severe and sensible: skirts no longer dragged on the ground, necks were higher, and sleeves, for the most part, were elbow length.

Historical Survey

NINTH CENTURY THROUGH THIRTEENTH CENTURY

800: Charlemagne (Charles I, 742-814), King of the Franks and emperor of the West, crowned Holy Roman Emperor by Pope Leo III.

828: All of England united for the first time, under Egbert (755?-839).

897: Alfred the Great (849-99), King of the West Saxons, built navy and defeated the invading Danes; thereafter consolidated all England around his kingdom.

962: Otto I, King of the Germans, crowned Holy Roman Emperor (first Saxon emperor) by Pope John XII.

987: Hugh Capet elected nominal King of France by the nobles.

1017: Canute II, King of the Danes, chosen king after conquering England.

1066: William I (the Conqueror, 1027-87), Duke of Normandy, led the Norman invasion of England.

1077: Henry IV, King of Germany and Holy Roman Emperor (1056-1106), humiliated himself before Pope Gregory VII at Canossa.

1095: Pope Urban II, at Clermont, summoned the First Crusade.

1099: Jerusalem captured from the Seljuks by the People's (First) Crusade.

c. 1110: Founding of Cambridge University.

1155: Frederick I (Barbarossa) crowned Holy Roman Emperor.

1187: Jerusalem captured by Saladin (1138-93), Sultan of Egypt and Syria.

1189-90: Start of the Third Crusade, led by Richard I (Coeur de Lion, 1157-99), King of England, and Philip II (1165-1223), King of France.

1198: Election of Innocent III as pope. During his reign (to 1216) papal power was at its highest.

1200: University of Paris chartered.

1202-04: Normandy and several other English provinces in France conquered by Philip II of France.

1204: Constantinople captured by members of the Fourth Crusade.

1215: Magna Charta signed by King John, under pressure by English barons.
Dominican order founded by (Saint) Dominic (1170-1221).

1226: Death of (Saint) Francis of Assisi (born 1182), founder of the Franciscan order.

1238: Granada established as the capital of an independent Moorish kingdom.

1244: Jerusalem recaptured by Egyptian Sultan.

1274: Death of Thomas Aquinas (born c. 1225), Italian Dominican philosopher and theologian.

1294: Death of Roger Bacon (born c. 1214), English philosopher and first experimental scientist, possibly the inventor of gunpowder.

1295: First English parliament, at Westminster.
Marco Polo (1254?-1324?), Venetian traveler in the Far East, returned from the court of Kublai Khan, allegedly bearing two important inventions: gunpowder and spaghetti.

1298: Foundation of the Duomo, in Florence.

People of the ninth century

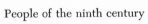

Carolingian man

King David

From a MS

Lower classes, eleventh century

23

Hunter

From Chartres Cathedral

1380

1310

Henry IV

English nobles

Horseman

1250

English official

1210

Commoner

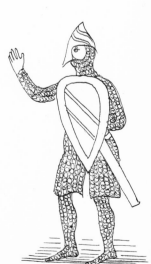

Soldier

Historical Survey

1300 TO 1485

1302: First French parliament, the States-General, established by Philip IV (King of France 1285-1314).

c. 1303: Giotto (1274?-1337?), Florentine painter, sculptor, and architect, began frescoes for Chapel of the Arena in Padua.

c. 1307: *Divine Comedy* begun by Dante Alighieri (1265-1321), Italian poet.

1308-11: Altarpiece for the Cathedral of Siena by Duccio di Buoninsegna (1255?-1319?), Italian painter of the Sienese school.

1326: First mention of the use of gunpowder (in Venice) for warfare.

1327: Petrarch (1304-74), Italian poet, met "Laura," to whom his *Canzoniere* were written.

1337: Beginning of Hundred Years' War between England and France.

1348: The Black Death, a virulent form of plague that decimated Western Europe, reached England.

1353: The *Decameron*, by Giovanni Boccaccio (1313-75), Italian writer.

1358: The *Jacquerie*, French peasant revolt, led by Jacques Bonhomme against the nobles.

1378: Start of the Western Schism, breach in the Western Church caused by the disputed election of Pope Urban VI.

1381: Murder of Wat Tyler, leader of the Peasants' Revolt in England, who protested against the Statute of Laborers, poll tax, and economic hardships.

Genoa defeated by Venice; beginning of the greatness of the Venetian Republic.

1386-1400: *Canterbury Tales*, by Geoffrey Chaucer (1340?-1400), English poet.

c. 1388: First complete translation of the Bible, by John Wycliff (1320?-84), English religious reformer.

1415: Battle of Agincourt; French defeated by Henry V of England.

1415: John Huss, Bohemian religious reformer influenced by Wycliff, burned at the stake for heresy.

1417: End of the Western Schism with the election of Martin V, Pope from 1417-31.

1424-25: Lorenzo Ghiberti (1378-1455), Florentine painter and sculptor, finished north bronze doors for Baptistery at Florence and began east doors.

1429: Siege of Orléans raised by Joan of Arc (1412-31), who led French troops against the English and was instrumental in the crowning of the dauphin as Charles VII in the same year.

1430: Bronze "David" executed for the Medici Palace in Florence by Donatello (1386?-1466), leader in early Renaissance sculpture.

1431-38: Singing gallery panel for Cathedral Museum, Florence, by Luca della Robbia (1400?-82), Florentine sculptor.

1434: "Giovanni Arnolfini and His Wife," by Jan von Eyck (1370?-1440?), Flemish painter.

c. 1450: "Etienne Chevalier and St. Stephen," by Jean Fouquet (1416?-80), French painter.

1453: End of Hundred Years' War; English expelled from all of France but Calais.
Fall of Constantinople to the Turks, bringing the Byzantine empire to an end.

1455: Beginning of Wars of the Roses, civil war in England between the houses of Lancaster and York.

c. 1456: First Bible printed by Johann Gutenberg (1400?-68?), German inventor of movable type.

1459: "Journey of the Magi" begun for chapel of the Medici palace in Florence by Benozzo Gozzoli (1420-98), Florentine painter.

1460: Death of Henry the Navigator (born 1394), Prince of Portugal and patron of navigation and exploration.

1461: *Le Grand Testament,* by François Villon (born 1431), French poet and one of the greatest French lyricists.

1469: Lorenzo de' Medici (1449-92) became head of the powerful de' Medici family.
Marriage of Ferdinand of Aragon and Isabella of Castile, paving the way for the union of the two kingdoms in 1479.

1471: Edward IV (1442-83), King of England, re-established the dynasty of the house of York.

1476: First known printing in England done by William Caxton (1422?-91).

c. 1478: "Spring," by Sandro Botticelli (1444?-1510), Italian painter.

1480-81: Maine, Provence, Anjou, and other French provinces united with the crown under Louis XI, laying the foundation for an absolute monarchy.

1485-90: "The Hay Wagon," by Hieronymus Bosch, Dutch painter.

1485: End of Wars of the Roses; battle of Bosworth Field, in which Richard III was defeated and killed by the Earl of Richmond, later Henry VII, first of the Tudors.

Entertainer   King Arthur   Entertainer

These figures from the Hero's Tapestry, Cloisters

French courtiers

French nobles

All this page from *Les très riches heures du Duc de Berri*

Upper-class German ladies

Noble lady

Italian gentleman

Noble lady

Two upper-class Germans

German commoner

German gentleman

Noble German ladies

German courtiers

Figures on this page after the Master of E.S., German engraver

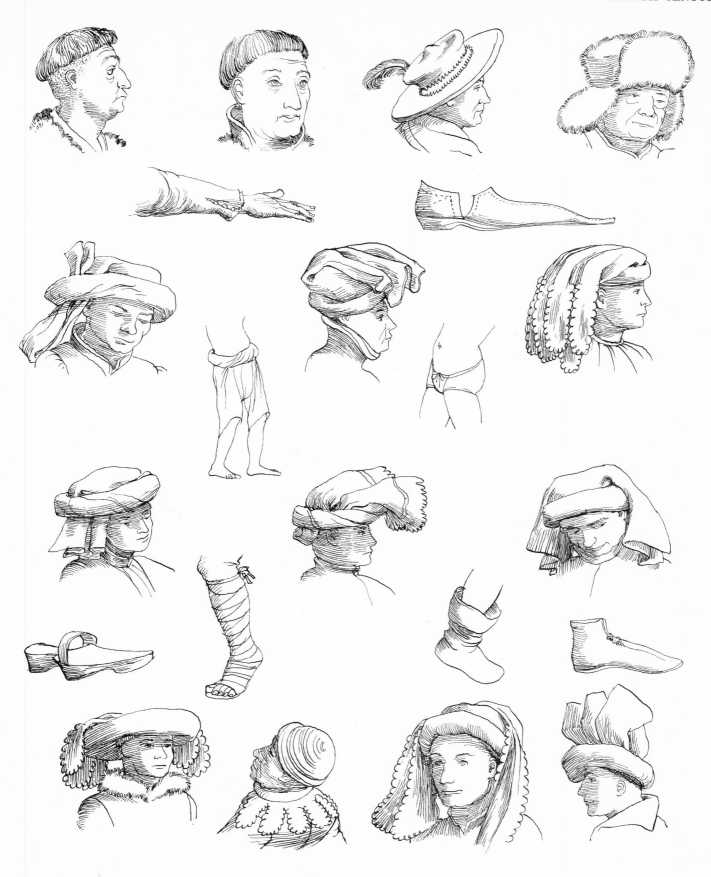

Details from *Joan of Arc* by Adrien Harmand

Figures from a Flemish tapestry

Figures from the Unicorn Tapestries, French

Spanish   German   French   German

Hunter

Slashings

Flemish shoe

Armor

EUROPEAN ARMOR evolved roughly over the thousand years from 650 to 1650, but in the defensive accouterment of ancient peoples can be found the forerunner for practically everything later developed. Not only Greek and Roman influences can be traced, but Etruscan, Celtic, and Byzantine. Etruscan bronze helmets, for example, date from well before the twelfth century B.C.

Defensive armor in the early feudal period was not elaborate. The knight's lower legs were unprotected. Over his torso he wore a hawberk, or tunic, of chain mail slashed at the bottom to fasten about the thigh. A conical steel helmet with a nose guard protected his face. He carried a kite-shaped shield about four feet long.

It must be remembered that armor was, on the whole, the prerogative of the upper classes. The suits of steel commonly seen in museums were worn only by the greatest and wealthiest of lords, and rarely, if at all, by the common fighting men of the Middle Ages. The ordinary soldier was fortunate if he had a tunic of mail and a steel cap. Many of those who aspired to knighthood had to remain squires, or servants to knights, because of their inability to afford the chivalric glory of full armor.

Beginning with the twelfth century, chain mail was gradually extended to include hood and hose, clothing the knight from head to foot. Under the mail was a gambeson, and over it a pourpoint, both made of leather or quilted fabric. The problem of distinguishing friend from foe, when both were completely encased in steel, was solved by the introduction, in the twelfth century, of amorial bearings, which laid the foundation for the great arts and skills of heraldry.

During the thirteenth century chain mail was gradually reinforced by plates at strategic points, beginning with the chest region. The great helm was common, but its use was reserved chiefly for tournaments and display. In battle the knight wore a mail hood with a steel cap either over or under it. Helms were of great variety, some flat or round-topped with a hinged or movable ventaile (to admit air), and others in one piece, pierced for eye holes. At the end of the century the sugarloaf shape of helm was introduced.

By the fourteenth century the knight was entirely encased in plate metal having articulated joints. The characteristic helmet of this time was the salade, a large steel cap visored all around. The toes of metal shoes were sharply pointed.

Armor of the fifteenth century was simpler in construction and therefore somewhat lighter in weight. A shirt of light mail was worn as additional protection under the plate. As this century progressed, however, armor ceased to be functional and began to imitate civilian clothing.

The sixteenth century continued this trend and in addition emphasized decoration; surface etching and inlay provided the final corruption of the beautiful lines and utility of earlier armor. Incidentally, the decoration of armor gave impetus to the art of etching. The introduction of gunpowder doomed utilitarian armor. At first, in order to protect the wearer against powder-driven shot, armor was made heavier, but, as its weight became impractical, it was gradually abandoned. This transition period, during which firearms were becoming practical weapons and the armorer was concerned chiefly with ostentatious display, lasted into the seventeenth century. After that time the preoccupations of fighting men were devoted to weapons of offense rather than of defense.

Eleventh century

Ninth century

Twelfth century

French, fourteenth century

1400

Italian, fifteenth century

1290

Late thirteenth century

1340

1200

1075

1360

French armor, eleventh to fourteenth centuries

Tilting suit   Crossbowman   Tilting suit

c.1530   1460   c.1530

1375   1461   c.1380

French armor of the fourteenth and fifteenth centuries

1450   1460   1380   1460

Various military services of the fourteenth and fifteenth centuries

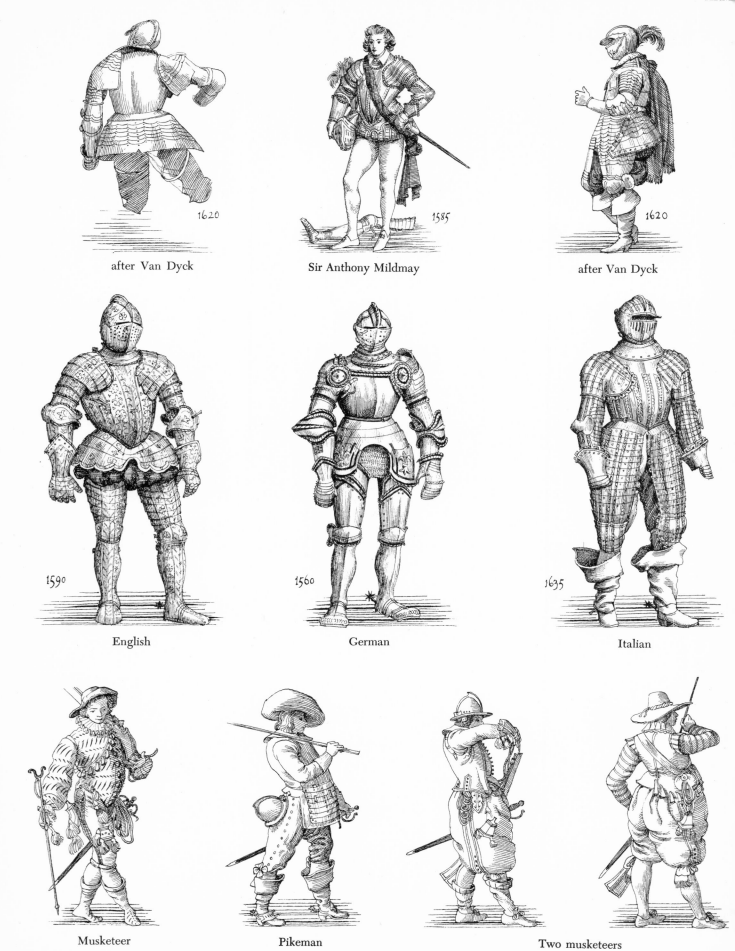

after Van Dyck

1620

Sir Anthony Mildmay

1585

after Van Dyck

1620

English

1590

German

1560

Italian

1635

Musketeer

Pikeman

Two musketeers

HENRY VIII, AFTER HOLBEIN

The Tudor Period (1485-1603)

HENRY VII's reign (1485-1509) ushered in an entirely new era, and for the first time we begin to sense some of the more "modern" atmosphere, suggesting bankers and countinghouses. There was a vast increase in printing, and paper was easily available after the fourteenth century. As knowledge was more widely disseminated, the spirit of inquiry developed and spread, leading to the religious and intellectual revolts culminating in the Reformation. Feudalism had largely disappeared. Craft guilds had become capitalistic enterprises, and commercial competition was increasing. Society was faced with problems that are still prevalent today: those of relationship between classes.

Style centers shifted from country to country throughout Europe. In the first part of the century the German-Swiss influence was predominant — this, in turn, derived from Italy — and in the latter part the foremost style center was Spain.

The English, the men even more than the women, followed each new style with delight. Among the upper classes men and women shared equally in the color and splendor of clothing. Sixteenth-century England broke with the past in the matter of dress as well as in social attitudes. Men's clothing was entirely new except for hose and codpiece, and the latter became increasingly evident. Doublet and jerkin were very tailored. The neck of the doublet gradually grew higher and became collarlike, while the shirt neckline began its transformation into the ruff. Sleeves were wide and slashed but fitted tightly at the wrist. Later, hose were converted into two distinct garments: above, slashed and puffed breeches; below, stockings. Shoes were also slashed, and they were often decorated. Later they broadened at the toes to form the shovel shape associated wtih Henry VIII. Low-crowned, brimmed bonnets, nicked at one side, carried plumes; but later the plumes decreased in number and brims narrowed. Cloaks were often fur-lined. Those worn by dignitaries, with puffed and slashed sleeves, descended to the ankles.

Among women, the spectacular headdresses of the preceding age had been discarded in favor of the hood, which covered head and shoulders, its gabled front edged with a broad, stiff band of needlework and its ends falling in lappets to the breast. Gowns were rather stern and simple, with tight-fitting, long-waisted bodices and long skirts which flared at the hips and fell to the ground. Sleeves were wide and turned back to form a cuff, often of fur. A loose girdle encircled a low waistline, and from it pendants dangled to the floor. A long cloak was tied at the neck with long dangling cords, as illustrated.

The middle part of the Tudor period inevitably reflected the taste and character of Henry VIII, the king so outstanding in many respects that even today we tend to associate the period with the man rather than the reverse. Henry VIII was proud of his broad shoulders, and it is not surprising that the style of clothing he adopted emphasized and exaggerated this feature; many of his portraits show his torso as almost square, as broad as it is long. The king's luxurious tastes and love of finery were expressed through use of cloth of gold, velvet, silk, lace, damask, furs, and jewels. A short, high-collared doublet was either slashed or open at the front to show the embroidered undershirt, which was ruffled at the wrists. Covering the doublet was an overjerkin with exaggerated puffed sleeves. These sleeves were still long, as they had been in earlier times, but the hanging portion had been separated from the actual sleeve and had become largely functionless; from the middle of the sixteenth century to the eighteenth century such sleeves were little more than another portion of clothing that could be lavishly decorated and embroidered. The upper legs were covered by breeches cut almost as full as "bloomers" and sometimes padded.

Circling the stockings below the knees were decorative garters. The shovel shoe introduced by Henry VIII has already been mentioned; at the height of its fashion it was reproduced even in armor. Men were mustached and bearded, but they followed the French custom of cropping the hair. The flat velvet or fur cap had lost its nicked edge and its plumes; by this time it usually had a plume draped about its low crown. The cap was worn tilted, thus exposing the heavily jeweled underside. Sword and dagger were everyday accessories.

Women's clothing in general followed men's patterns, but since their anatomies did not lend themselves to the square torso, the German influence is less noticeable. Gowns and petticoats were of stiff silk. Necklines were low-cut and somewhat square, but they gradually became yokes and then high collars. Headdresses consisted of hoods and caps or some combination of the two.

Under Edward VI (reigned 1547-1553) and Mary Tudor (reigned 1553-1558) clothing lost the ornate decorative detail of the earlier part of the period. The sumptuary laws proclaimed by Mary were directed against rich apparel and jewelry for the rising middle classes, and we find clothing generally rather plain. Among the upper classes, the skirts of women's gowns spread out stiffly from a tight waist and were opened in front as an inverted V to show the heavy embroidered silk petticoat beneath. French hoods (off-the-face caps stiffened with wires) and velvet bonnets were worn on the head. The large puff where the sleeve joined the shoulder was the most elaborate and characteristic detail of the period; this same style appeared in clothing of both men and women. Shoes were again narrow. The necklines of gowns and undergarments were rising, foreshadowing the ruffs at neck and wrist which were to become one of the most typical and exaggerated elements of Elizabethan dress.

By the time of Elizabeth the square, stubby truculence of Henry VIII had completely disappeared and we find the English, especially, but also the French beginning to have the appearance that we think of as Elizabethan. In one field the adventurous magnificence of Drake was at its height, and in another, the vibrant creativeness of Shakespeare and other writers. Those qualities which were to detach England increasingly from the Continent became more pronounced. One senses in English costumes the individualism of English thought. The Italians, Spanish, and French were clinging to a more romantic and noble grace; and German styles, as usual, were somewhat ugly and fantastic.

During the reign of Elizabeth (1558-1603) clothes became models of confinement. Elizabeth herself — tiny, slender, vain, extravagant — was the sole arbiter of style, as her father, Henry VIII, had been in his time. Women's clothing set the styles, and men's copied it. The outstanding characteristic was the ruff. Women wore immense cambric collars, ruffle piled on ruffle in fan or cartwheel shape, not only starched but wired and trussed to present the proper strangulating appearance. Hair (or sometimes wig, as in Elizabeth's case) was elaborately curled and raised high in a jeweled wire frame, and from the headdress wide sprays of wired veiling extended at each side. The line of the upper torso was extended well below the waist as a stuffed or quilted V shape. Corsets had been worn since the early part of the sixteenth century. At that time they were rigid hinged iron; later they were made of flexible steel, and in the late part of the century were boned fabric. For some time skirts had been flared by means of funnel-shaped Spanish farthingales, and after 1570 they jutted out stiffly from the hips, which were padded by great folds of cloth, creating cylinder or drum shapes. These exaggerated styles caused court gentle-women to resemble tops or fantastic kites. Cosmetics were very common, and lace was rather widely used. Masks were affected by both men and women. From their embroidered high-heeled shoes to their painted faces and dyed locks, frizzled and eked out with the "curl'd-worne tresses of dead-borrowed haire," the fashionable ladies of the late 1500s were the epitome of artificiality.

Men wore ruffs both at neck and wrist. In general doublets followed the line of women's bodices. Capes were long or short, with or without sleeves. The codpiece disappeared during the latter part of the century. Long hose had by this time become upper breeches, boned and padded at the hips (similar to the effect produced by women's rolls and hoops); and stockings. Knitted silk stockings were introduced, and the garter was increasingly an item of high style. Shoes were narrow and slitted. Late in the century high heels appeared. Gauntlet gloves were used widely.

Both men and women wore ornate jewelry. Elizabeth herself had a great penchant for draped strands of pearls, large elaborate pendants, jeweled hat bands, bracelets, rings, and earrings. Men as well as women wore earrings.

Apart from court dress, clothing continued to be utilitarian and plain. The beginnings of Puritanism had sobered the middle classes, and the great mass of people remained sensibly clothed.

Historical Survey

1485: Beginning of the reign of Henry VII in England, first Tudor king.

1486: Bartholomeu Dias (1450?-1500) rounded the Cape of Good Hope, opening a route to the East.

1492: Conquest of Granada, the last Moorish stronghold in Spain.

First voyage of Columbus (1466?-1506) to the New World.

1494-98: "The Last Supper" painted by Leonardo da Vinci (1452-1519), Florentine painter, sculptor, architect, engineer, and scientist.

1498: Savonarola, Florentine reformer, burned as a heretic.

Vasco da Gama made the first voyage from Western Europe around Africa to the East.

1501: *In Praise of Folly*, by Erasmus (1466?-1536).

1508: "The Judgment of Paris," by Lucas Cranach the Elder (1472-1553), German painter and woodcut designer.

1508-12: Michelangelo (1475-1564), Italian sculptor, painter, architect, and poet, painted the Sistine Chapel ceiling frescoes.

1509: Beginning of the reign of Henry VIII of England (1491-1547).

1509-11: "Stanza della Segnature" fresco by Raphael (1483-1520), Italian painter.

c. 1510-12: "The Sacred and Profane Love," by Titian (1477-1576), Italian painter of the Venetian school.

1513: Vasco Nuñez de Balboa (1475-1517) discovered the Pacific Ocean.

The Prince, by Niccolo Machiavelli.

"The Knight and Death," copper engraving by Albrecht Dürer (1471-1528), German painter and engraver.

c. 1515: Isenheim altarpiece completed by Matthias Grünewald (1500-30), German painter.

1517: The Ninety-five Theses of Martin Luther (1483-1546).

1519-21: Conquest of Mexico by Hernando Cortes (1485-1547).

1519-22: Ferdinand Magellan (1480?-1521) sailed through the Strait of Magellan, discovered the Philippines, and was killed; but one of his ships completed the first circumnavigation of the world.

c. 1530: Nicolaus Copernicus (1473-1543) wrote *De Revolutionibus Orbium Coelestium.*

1534: Founding of Jesuit order by Saint Ignatius of Loyola (1491-1556).

c. 1534: Henry VIII's Act of Supremacy created a national church in England.

Gargantua, by François Rabelais (1494?-1553).

1536: John Calvin (1509-64) published *Institutes of the Christian Religion.*

1536-39: Monasteries in England suppressed by Henry VIII.

c. 1537: "Henry VIII," by Hans Holbein the Younger (1497?-1543), German painter.

1545: Council of Trent reiterated papal authority and outlined Catholic orthodoxy.

1548: "The Miracle of St. Mark," by Il Tintoretto (1518-94), painter of the Venetian school.

Upper-class Flemish people

French lady

German capitalist

Flemish lady

Flemish workmen

Flemish nobles

These figures from Franco-Flemish tapestry

Details of early sixteenth-century dress

Flemish countryfolk

German lady   1517

German warrior   1530

1520   German lady

German gentleman   1525

1528   English lady with rosary   1528

1525   German lady

Flemish peasants

1536 Italian lady

English lady 1528

French ambassador 1533

1538 Queen Christina of Denmark

Flemish peasant

Italian gentleman 1525

French bishop 1533

Flemish peasant

Early sixteenth-century headgear

Three upper-class Germans, after Cranach

1554

Queen Mary

1550

English gentleman

1555

after Pourbus

1545

1550

1543

Upper-class citizens, after Hans Mielich

Mid-century Tudor headgear

German gentleman

Duke Henry the Pious, after Cranach

German lady

English lady

German gentleman

Anne of Denmark

German gentleman

Martin Luther

German gentleman

Spanish gentleman

Historical Survey

LATE TUDOR PERIOD (1558-1603)

1558: Elizabeth (1533-1603) became Queen of England.
Benvenuto Cellini (1500-71) started his *Autobiography*.

1560: *Treatise on Predestination,* by John Knox (1502-72).

1563: "Marriage at Cana" painted by Paolo Veronese (1528-88), of the Venetian School.

1566: "The Wedding Dance," by Peter Brueghel the Elder (1520?-69), Flemish painter.

1567: *Pope Marcellus Mass,* by Palestrina (1526?-94).

1572: Massacre of St. Bartholomew, in France.

1579: Dutch Republic established under William the Silent (1533-84).

1587: Mary, Queen of Scots, beheaded by order of Elizabeth.

1588: Spanish Armada, sent against England by Philip II of Spain (1527-98), defeated.
Third book of *Essays* by Montaigne (1533-92).

1590: *The Faerie Queene,* books 1-3, by Edmund Spenser (1552?-99).

1597: First *Essays* by Francis Bacon (1561-1626).

1598: Edict of Nantes issued by Henry IV of France (1553-1610), giving Huguenots and Catholics equality before the law.

1600: First charter granted to the English East India Company.

1600-1601: "View of Toledo," by El Greco (1548-1614?), Cretan-born painter of the Castilian school.

1603: Death of Elizabeth.

Italian gentleman

German prince
1564

English lady
1576

Gentlemen
1567   1567

Noble lady
1567

Official
c.1560

Italian gentleman

Gentleman
1560

Italian lady

Italian lady, after Moroni

Spanish lady

Gentleman, after Moro

German lady

Sir Martin Frobisher

Queen Anne of Spain

Fashionable Frenchman

Italian gentleman

Italian gentleman

Charles IX of France

57

Details of late Tudor dress   Shoe and sleeve, after Titian

James I as a boy

1585

Henry III

c. 1580

English lady

1589

Ann of Boskovic

1588

Earl of Leicester

1593

Queen Elizabeth

1592

after Pourbus

Queen Elizabeth

1593

Two court figures

Elizabethan vanities

1580   1580

Three Italian ladies

1580   1588   1581

Italian lady   Sir Walter Raleigh   Italian lady

c.1580   1587   1580   1587

English gentleman   Three German gentlefolk

Sir Philip Sidney

1585

French lady

Sir Walter Raleigh

1581

French lady

1588

Queen Elizabeth

1580

English lady

Widow

Sir John Hawkins

after Zuccaro

Duke de Guise

FASHIONABLE LADY, AFTER WENZEL HOLLAR

The Seventeenth Century

THE ELIZABETHAN style of dress continued into the seventeenth century under James I in England and Louis XIII in France. Men wore a tight, one-piece doublet with short skirts and tightly cut sleeves. Padded and puffed breeches were still the mode, but during the early 1700s they became fuller and looser, often open-bottomed. Later in the century this trend was reversed and they were again narrower, reminiscent of shorts. Boots often had colored linings made of delicate materials. Men's hats, of felt or beaver, were large, cylindrical or conical in shape, and lavishly decorated. Hair was worn long, but beards became the "Vandyke."

At the turn of the century women's clothing was still under Spanish influence, including the farthingale, a very ugly garment. Ruff and bodice were again cut away to reveal the bosom. Underskirts were ground length. Though women were becoming more feminine in their clothing, they followed men's styles of hair dressing and wore men's high-crowned hats.

Both ladies and gentlemen wore silk stockings, which by this time were being woven mechanically. Clothes for both sexes were decorated with lace, ribbons, embroidery, artificial flowers, quiltings, and jewels.

During the reign of Charles I (1625-1649), as the differences between the Crown and Parliament increased and became critical in England, the clothing of the period also separated into two widely dissimilar and irreconcilable styles. On the one hand was the garb of the middle-class Puritan dissenter who, as an expression of moral and political disapproval, adopted a black, wide-brimmed, high-crowned felt hat worn over short-clipped hair; a somber coat slightly relieved at the neckline by the wide, plain collar of the shirt; and woolen stockings. Womens' dress corresponded, save that their dark gowns revealed stiff underskirts. This same influence may be seen in a more sophisticated form in the Dutch clothing illustrated here.

On the other hand there was the dress of cavaliers and their ladies, famed for its magnificence. The familiar paintings of Van Dyck have mirrored the styles then prevalent among the upper classes. Men's hats were boldly feathered; their doublets revealed great expanses of white linen shirting, laced at neck and wrist; fabrics were rich and elegant. Ruffs had given place to a casual, wide, falling collar of linen or lace over the shoulders. Hair was worn long, and a lovelock fell loosely at one side. Breeches were shorter, narrower, and fringed. Boot tops were loose and full; during the Thirty Years' War (1618-1648) men invariably wore boots and spurs, as well as leather jerkins, plumed and cocked military hats, and cloaks, thus giving rise to a distinct "cavalier" style, represented in France by the Three Musketeers. The doublet, in process of transformation to a coat, became shorter.

Paddings and slashings were in large part abandoned by women, and clothing became extremely loose and casual. Long series of richly laced collars sloped down over the shoulders. A sort of vest was cut to reveal a great expanse of bosom. Sleeves were wide, elbow length, with a laced cuff; the skirt was full. The hair was dressed casually, as though rumpled in the course of some game.

The artist Rubens (1577-1640) vividly pictured the Spanish-dominated northern Flemish world. He delighted in dressing his models elaborately and painting them, bursting out of the latest fashions, with the warmest appreciation of their natures. Never has the femininity of women been more ardently espoused than by Rubens. This is not to overlook the charming satire of Jan van de Velde (to 1630), which points out so clearly the ludicrousness of these fashions which in another, greater, artist's hands had the appearance of magnificence.

Rembrandt's Holland, though it followed similar styles, was much more decorous and puritanical in mood. The high fashions of France, judged from Bosse's engravings, were stiffer and more awkward.

The lovely bloom of Dutch genre painting shows us more of middle-class costume than we have seen in former periods. Holland was the very citadel of the rising capitalist middle class, and her artists delighted in portraying people as they were: homely, sincere, and bourgeois. De Hooch, Terborch, and Vermeer are especially instructive. Jan Steen shows us the tavern frolic, the lusty dissipations of a merchant people. Just as we tend to associate the Frenchman of the period with his rapier, we should think of the Dutchman hurling a tankard at his enemy.

In the latter part of the century, Charles II (reigned 1660-1685) brought back to England the extravagant French costume of Louis XIV's court, to rout the Puritan collar. At the time of his return men's clothing consisted of a short-waisted doublet with loose, slashed sleeves; short, wide petticoat breeches; and full stocking hose that draped over the garter. Charles's influence added, in the fashion of French courtiers, rows of looped ribbons to the "rhinegrave" breeches, drooping ruffles at the knees, and plumes to the hat. The cocked hats of earlier decades became tricornes in the '90s. Boots were displaced by shoes with stiff bows. As these became lighter in weight, heels grew higher.

About 1665 the "vest" was introduced as a variant of the doublet, first with sleeves and later sleeveless. With this addition, men's dress became identifiable with that of the present day: a rather straight, thigh-length coat, waist-length vest, and breeches.

The other outstanding innovation of the period was the wig or peruke or periwig for all men of substance, a style that was to last for over a century. By the end of the century the wig reached its greatest dimensions, cascading in curls over the shoulders or even below. (In the home it was replaced by an embroidered or furred cap or nightcap.) The cloak was rarely seen by now, and the coat was well established as an essential of dress. It was often worn open so as to show the vest beneath. A large cravat, its ends laced, was usually tied at the neck and sometimes was slipped into the opening of the vest.

Women's gowns of the late seventeenth century were long-waisted and closely cut. Sleeves were loose, turned back at the elbows; and a wide collar covered the shoulders. After 1660 the loose overskirt was drawn back and up, as the curtains of a stage would be lifted, gradually revealing the full underskirt in front, while the overskirt became a sort of bustle draped behind. Over the skirt a small lace apron was often worn. Caps with long lace lappets appeared; or a loose hood covered the head out of doors. The long-handled parasol was practically obligatory by 1680, as may be seen in the illustrations. For riding or walking, ladies aped their gentlemen in coat, waistcoat, hat, and cravat.

From their elaborately coifed headdresses to their decorative feet, the upper-class women constantly demonstrated to the fashionable world — and to the lower classes — that they could not possibly do the slightest labor. One must assume that this has been one of the most important factors dictating the history of fashion. It is certain that exaggerated styles, whenever and wherever they have occurred, were symptomatic of the attitudes of the times: a flaunting of one's idleness; ostentation; and a clear statement of wealth as well as nobility of birth.

Upper-class men — mannered, artificial, dandified, occupied with their snuff boxes, handkerchiefs, canes, gloves, muffs, paint, patches, and perfume — seem a very far cry from the reasonably familiar figure of the nineteenth-century American. During the 1600s and 1700s men's clothing far outshone women's in color, design, and elaborateness. This is curiously at variance with our present fashions of sober, uniform, unimaginative men's clothing.

Historical Survey

EARLY SEVENTEENTH CENTURY (1600-1645)

1603: Beginning of the reign of James I (1566-1625), first Stuart king.

1605: *Volpone,* by Ben Jonson (1573?-1637), English playwright and poet.

1605-06: *Macbeth,* by William Shakespeare (1564-1616); the first decade of the century marked his greatest and most productive period.

1606: Part I of *Don Quixote,* by Miguel de Cervantes Saavedra (1547-1616), Spanish novelist.

1607: Captain John Smith (1580-1631) established the first permanent English settlement in America at Jamestown, Va.
Orfeo, opera by Monteverdi (1567-1643), Italian composer.

1609: Johannes Kepler (1571-1630), German astronomer, propounded his first two laws of planetary motion.
Henry Hudson (died 1611), English navigator for the Dutch East India Company, sailed the *Half Moon* into New York harbor and up the river; established a trading post on Manhattan.

1611: Publication of the King James Bible.

1613: Galileo Galilei (1564-1642), Italian astronomer, was denounced for the heretical views of his *Letters on the Solar Spots,* in which he advocated the Copernican system. Later, after trial by the Inquisition, he recanted.

1618: Outbreak of the Thirty Years' War between Catholics and Protestants; originated in Germany but involved most of Western Europe.

Cycle of Holy Sonnets, by John Donne (1573-1631), English metaphysical poet.

1620: Arrival of Pilgrims at Plymouth, in the *Mayflower.* First Negro slaves brought into the Jamestown colony.

Novum Organum, by Francis Bacon (1561-1626), English philosopher and author.

1621: *Anatomy of Melancholy,* by Robert Burton (1577-1640), English clergyman.

c. 1622: "Marie de' Medici" series finished by Peter Paul Rubens (1577-1640), Flemish painter.

1626: Peter Minuit purchased Manhattan from the Indians.

1628: *Essay on the Motion of the Heart and the Blood,* by William Harvey (1578-1657), English physician and anatomist.

1629: Cardinal Richelieu (1585-1642) officially appointed prime minister of France; dictated national policies until his death.

"Los Borrachos," by Velázquez (1599-1660), Spanish painter.

1635: "Charles I," by Sir Anthony Van Dyck (1599-1641), Flemish painter.

1636: Founding of Harvard College, first institution of learning in America.

1637: *Discourse on Method,* by René Descartes (1596-1650), French scientist and philosopher.

1638-39: "Et in Arcadia Ego," by Nicolas Poussain (1594-1665), French historical and landscape painter.

1642: Charles I started war against the Puritan Parliament (Long Parliament); led to civil war, the Great Rebellion, 1642-49.

"The Night Watch," by Rembrandt van Rijn (1606-69), Dutch painter and etcher.

1610   1610   1611

1620   1613

1619

Early seventeenth-century headgear

1610   1620   1615   1605   Breeches   Spanish sleeve
1615   1600   1590   1600

Lady, after Merian   Louis XIII   English lady

Dutch lady   English gentleman   English lady

Dutch gentleman   Dutch citizen   German gentleman   Dutch gentleman

The exposed fashion   Two Dutch ladies

Dutch lady   Charles I of England   Dutch lady

Four Dutch citizens of the mercantile class

1630

1625

1628

1624

1628

1630

1625

1621

Details of dress

1628

1625

1627

1625

1625

1629

Boots and spurs

Page

Noble youth

Princess of Nassau-Orange

Lady, after Van Dyck

Marquis of Hamilton

French lady

French, Dutch, French, and English gentlemen

Miss Herbert

Beatrice de Cusance

Queen Henrietta Maria

Noble lady

Sir Thomas Wharton

Noble lady

Sir A. Goodwin

Viscount Grandison

Lord Bernard Stuart

William II of Orange

75

French lady

French gentleman

Dutch lady

Rubens' wife

Gentleman, after Maes

Flemish lady

Four gentlemen

Three French ladies

French lady

Dutch burghers, after Rembrandt

Two French gentlemen

English gentleman

Dutch burgher

1635

1635

Details of dress

1630

1635

Hose   Sword hilt   Purse

Historical Survey

MIDDLE SEVENTEENTH CENTURY (1645-1665)

1646: "The Ecstasy of Santa Teresa," by Giovanni Lorenzo Bernini (1598-1680), Italian sculptor, painter, and architect.

1648: Thirty Years' War ended by Treaty of Westphalia: Alsace given to France; Netherlands and Switzerland became independent; Catholics and Protestants on equal basis.
Print, "Supper at Emmaus," by Rembrandt.
"Embarkation of the Queen of Sheba," by Claude Lorrain (1600-82), French landscape painter and engraver.

1649: Charles beheaded; England became a Commonwealth, ruled by Commons and a council of state. The office of the king and the House of Lords were abolished. Actual power was vested in Oliver Cromwell (1599-1658), who was installed as "Lord Protector" from 1653 until his death.

1656: "Las Meninas," by Velázquez.

1660: End of Commonwealth and restoration of the English monarchy with Charles II, a Stuart.
Beginning of Samuel Pepys' (1633-1703) *Diary*, maintained for almost ten years.

1661: Louis XIV (king 1643-1715) took control of the government upon the death of Cardinal Mazarin, French prime minister.

1663: Part 1 of *Hudibras*, by Samuel Butler (1612-80), English satirical poet.

1664: Nieuw Amsterdam captured by the British from the Dutch and renamed New York.
"Regents of the Old Men's Almshouse," by Frans Hals (1580?-1666), Dutch portrait and genre painter.

c. 1664: "The Lace Maker," by Jan Vermeer (1632-75), Dutch genre and portrait painter.

Mourning dress

English "anticke"

after Bolswert

French lady

James Stuart

Middle-class Dutch woman

English Roundhead

Three gentlemen

Flower girl

Upper-middle-class women

Spanish lady

French lady

Dutch lady

Fashionable street costumes

The mask fashion

Shoe with galosh

Muff

Patten

Details of mid-century dress

1663

1655

1659

Three Dutch women

1658

French lady

1650

1656

Two middle-class Dutch women

1650

Two French gentlemen

1653

Dutch soldier

1650

French gentleman

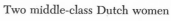

84

Historical Survey

LATE SEVENTEENTH CENTURY (1665-1700)

1666: *The Misanthrope,* by Molière (1622-73).

1667: Publication of *Paradise Lost,* by John Milton (1608-74), English poet.

1675: Sir Christopher Wren (1632-1723) started rebuilding St. Paul's Cathedral, destroyed by the Great Fire in London in 1666.

1677: *Phèdre,* by Jean Baptiste Racine (1639-99), French dramatic poet.

1678: *The Pilgrim's Progress,* by John Bunyan (1628-88), English preacher.
All for Love, by John Dryden (1631-1700), English poet.

1682: La Salle (1643-87) descended the Mississippi River and took possession of the river basin for Louis XIV.

1865: Edict of Nantes revoked by Louis XIV.

Beginning of reign of James II of England.

1687: Sir Isaac Newton (1642-1727) published *Principia,* formulating his laws of gravitation.

1688: The Glorious Revolution in England, followed by the accession of William III and Mary.

1689: Grand Alliance against France, by England, the Netherlands, the Holy Roman Empire, Spain, and Savoy, led to war, 1689-97.
Bill of Rights passed by the English Parliament.

c. 1689: *Dido and Aeneas,* opera by Henry Purcell (1659-95).

1699: First settlement in the Mississippi region, at Biloxi, Miss.

1660

1665

1660

1660

1660

1660

1663

1663

1665

Details of headgear

Shoes, boots, and slippers

1666

1665

House hat

Wrist lace

Lady

French gentleman, after Duchâtel

French gentleman

Dutch lady

Madame de Sévigné

Dutch lady

Three French gentlemen

Dutch gentleman

Dutch woman

French gentleman

Dutch woman

Three Dutch citizens

Middle-class Dutch citizens

1675

1678

1670

Whalebone bodice

1678

1672

1675

Bodice

c. 1670

House hat and nightcap

Mitten

Lace scarf

Lady and gentleman of the French nobility

Middle-class French woman

French lady

Dutch gentleman

French lady

Four middle-class Englishmen

French lady

after English carving

French lady

Three members of the French nobility

Three upper-class French people

Dutch gentleman

1688

1690

1688

1680

1690   1689   1684   1684

High French fashions of the '90s

French lady   French noble   French lady

Four French gentlemen

Negligee

Sleeves and cuffs

Hose   Garter

GAY PARISIANS, AFTER DEBUCOURT

The Eighteenth Century

PERHAPS the most distinctive aspects of eighteenth-century dress were women's headdresses and men's headgear. In the early 1700s women wore modest powdered wigs surmounted by hoods, but in mid-century they entered upon a phase of bizarre exaggeration that has never been equaled. During the early years of George III's reign (1760-1820) headdresses mounted upward, supported by frames or pads, until they attained incredible heights. To add to the effect, the topmost reaches were then feathered, beaded, curled, draped, and fantastically decorated, as with a ship in full sail. It was obviously impossible that these creations be devised by other than expert hairdressers — of which there were not many — and the latter part of the century was characterized by the pomaded, floured, filthy monstrosities that in other eras would have been termed extreme torture. One of the interesting by-products of these times was the slender ivory or wooden rod, heavily encrusted with jewels, with which milady would seek to dislodge vermin without disarranging the superstructure. The style was not as short-lived as one would imagine, but by 1790, well before the tax on flour imposed by Pitt during the shortages of 1795-1801, hair had lost its support and had gradually become a mass of ringlets worn loose in front and longer in back, as illustrated so charmingly in Debucourt's satirical etchings. This, in turn, was replaced by the small pseudo-Greek headdress characteristic of the classical revival near the turn of the century.

Another drastic and dramatic cycle was the size and shape of women's skirts. Though by 1700 the Spanish farthingale had been replaced by bustle and slight train, the middle eighteenth century saw a return of hoops as immoderate, in their way, as were women's headdresses. Hoops were now made of whalebone; they were circular in shape, gradually widening from waist to ankle. The resulting gowns were so large and cumbersome that doorways, stairways, and carriages had to be specially adapted to allow the woman of fashion to pass. This circular style was later replaced by two very wide panniers projecting laterally over the hips, as illustrated. This particular excess occurred at a period in which it balanced the heavy edifice atop a woman's head, and the problem of accommodating a gentle lady — jutting into the candelabra above and into the furniture below — must have taxed the social functions of the day. Late in the century hip panniers became smaller and finally changed into a back gather, or bustle, again illustrated by Debucourt.

Women's clothing was not immoderate throughout the entire century. During the reign of George II (1727-1760) there was a period of almost rural simplicity, especially in walking clothes, characterized by flat- or high-crowned hats and long dairymaid's aprons. A holdover from the seventeenth century was sacque, also called *robe à la française*. This was a loose gown, sometimes sleeveless, distinguished by two wide pleats or folds which fell from the shoulders to the floor without being held in at the waist (the Watteau back).

Women's bodices did not change much from those worn during the late seventeenth century. They were stiff, laced in front, cut in a low swoop which was filled with ruffles or folds. Sleeves were cuffed during the early part of the century and ruffled during the later part. Lace aprons, carried over from the 1600s, were very common for another fifty years.

Beginning with the '80s we see an engaging looseness of feminine attire, the bib crossed at the breasts, slyly revealing. It was a romantic period, late Gainsborough and Reynolds. The tall, feathered, guardsman-like hat was worn above loosely looped hair which sometimes fell in charming ringlets to the waist. In many ways this style, which continued into the '90s, with its large feathered sombrero at a rakish angle and charmingly demure gowns, is one of the most attractive and seductive of any era. It was satirized by Debucourt in the fantastic scene which we have reproduced.

By the 90's the bosom was emphasized by tied kerchiefs which made the wearer look like a pouter pigeon. Waistlines were very high, ending under the armpits: gowns were described as "a petticoat tied round the neck." By this time skirts for outdoor wear had become moderate, and even court dress had smaller panniers. Yet court attire, with full complement of hoops, ribbons, garlands, tassels, and bows, lasted well into the nineteenth century — until, indeed, George IV, that friend of Beau Brummell, outlawed the fashion.

As can be imagined, head coverings had to change often and drastically in order to accommodate the bizarre styles of hairdressing. A carry-over into the century was the lace cap with hanging lappets. In addition, there were the many styles for ceremonial attire, for formal daytime wear, for walking or riding, each rigidly prescribed by fashion. Later, when soaring hair came into style, caps for home wear were originated: the mob cap, with full crown and frills, fastened under the chin; and the fly cap, with sides resembling wings. About 1785 bonnets were made of leghorn straw, coalscuttle-shaped, decorated with ribbons and feathers. Still later, during the classical revival, poke bonnets made their appearance — bonnets with wide flaring brims or fronts shading the face.

Light, printed cottons imported from India, when they had first appeared in France in the mid-seventeenth century, had been seized upon avidly by French and English women. Though they were first worn by aristocrats, they spread rapidly to the bourgeoisie, and by the beginning of the eighteenth century were a common garment for home and even outdoor wear. By the latter part of the century a domestic cotton-weaving industry was well established in all Western European countries and led to a great flood of machine-produced, plain or printed muslin and cotton for gowns and accessories. At the same time silk, wool, and linen continued to be important fabrics.

During the almost idyllic years of the early 1700s accessories declined in importance. Later, however, they returned in full vigor and were of even greater luxuriousness. Metal buttons and buckles were even more noticeable than they had been in earlier periods. Scarfs, muffs, mitts and gloves of silk and leather, folding fans, purses, beautiful canes, watches and fobs: all these were essentials.

A classical revival, partly inspired by the painter David, began at the end of the eighteenth century, but since this is more properly associated with the nineteenth, it will be described in that section.

During the 1700s men's hats were more important than their manner of doing the hair. The tricorne, adopted from the French, which was just appearing at the end of the seventeenth century, continued in one form or another throughout most of the eighteenth. There was every variation of the style, with brims wider and not so wide, loops here and there, and finally the development of the cockade. One form of cockaded hat was the military style, turned up in front and at the back, which continued into the nineteenth century. Though there were periods in which hats bore gold or silver lace or were rather heavily plumed, feathers decreased to a small border around the edge and were later replaced by braid. Wigs continued in favor until nearly the end of the century, but gave way to lower, simpler ones: the full hair of the periwig was gradually drawn back from the face and tied in back, then braided and ribboned (the tie wig), or was worn as a long pigtail looped up into a silken bag not unlike women's snoods of recent years (the bagwig). This in turn gave way to the bob wig, made familiar by the engraving of Washington on a dollar bill. After 1775 there was a trend toward one's own hair, dressed like a wig, and by the '90s most men and women had completely given up powdering it, though some old-fashioned notables continued the practice. By the end of the century men's hair was usually tied simply at the nape of the neck.

Men's garments did not change radically during the century. In the first half coats were knee length and very full in the skirt, while the waistcoat or vest was somewhat shorter. The vest developed lapels in the late part of the century and became sleeveless and short, ending at the waist. In Bernard Picart's costume prints of this period we see the loose, casual drapings of the long coat and waistcoat, with the first of the small, low-crowned cocked hats.

About the time of George III (reigned 1760-1820) the corners of coats began to be cut away diagonally, giving garments a back-swept appearance. This trend became accentuated and developed into the swallow-tailed frock coat, in which form it persisted well into the nineteenth century; it is now memorialized in today's "tails." Simultaneously sleeves became longer and cuffs less conspicuous; and in time the cuff disappeared, usually replaced by the present style of coat sleeve ending in a slit either buttoned or pseudo-buttoned. Collars became higher and more prominent. Decorated fabrics and other ornamentation gradually decreased throughout the 1700s, and after the '80s plain tailored cloth was usually seen. However, ruffled linen jabots or frilled shirt fronts lightened the upper part of garments. As coat lines were slanted backward, breeches became more important. Culottes, or breeches, as illustrated here, were cut on the bias at the top to improve their fit, and the lower leg was also better fitted. Stockings with garters, which had covered the bottoms of breeches in mid-century, now were covered by the breeches. In all these developments we have the antecedents of the nineteenth-century suit.

By the '80s, with the winds of the French Revolution stirring the air, there was a sudden reversal in fashion's mad plunges. Powder, gold lace, tricornes, and bagwigs disappeared almost suddenly. Tight pantaloons (worn by the sans-culottes of the French Revolution) replaced breeches; calf-length boots of soft leather were worn instead of the flaring jackboots of earlier times. Shoes for formal wear became plain buckled pumps. Another style of headgear was developed in this period: the high-crowned, narrow-brimmed hat which became the forerunner of the recent opera hat. Men had become definitely more conservative in dress both at home and in the streets. Indeed, this period marked the beginning of a trend in men's wear which has continued uninterruptedly, one in which clothing has become increasingly sober, standardized, and negligible in comparison with women's frills and pleasures.

Historical Survey

EARLY EIGHTEENTH CENTURY (1700-1745)

1701: War of the Spanish Succession: Second Grand Alliance — England, the Netherlands, Austria, Prussia, and the Holy Roman Empire — against France and Spain.
Frederick I (1657-1713) became King of Prussia.

1702: Queen Anne of England began reign.

1711-12, 1714: Joseph Addison and Sir Richard Steele published *The Spectator.*

1712: *The Rape of the Lock,* by Alexander Pope (1688-1744).

1713-14: Treaty of Utrecht ended the War of the Spanish Succession.

1715: Beginning of the reign of Louis XV of France (1710-74).

1717: "Embarkation for the Island of Cythera," by Jean Antoine Watteau (1684-1721), French painter.

1719: *Robinson Crusoe,* by Daniel Defoe (1659?-1731).

1726: *Gulliver's Travels,* by Jonathan Swift (1667-1745).

1728: *The Beggar's Opera,* by John Gay (1685-1732).

1735: Plates for "The Rake's Progress," by William Hogarth (1697-1764).

1738: *B-Minor Mass* completed by Johann Sebastian Bach (1685-1750).

1740: War of the Austrian Succession: Austria against France, Prussia, and Spain.
Beginning of the reign of Frederick II (the Great, 1712-86), King of Prussia.
"The Blessing," by Jean Baptiste Siméon Chardin (1699-1779), French genre painter.

1742: *The Messiah,* oratorio by George Frederick Handel (1685-1759).

Upper-class French people

1706

1710

1700

Three gentlemen of the early eighteenth century

c. 1700

Four French gentlemen, after Picart

1704

1705

1704

1715

1720

1707

1717

1705

Hair styles and headdresses, 1700-20

1700

1715

Shoulder loops   Hose   Boned corset   Lace cap

Upper-class French people, after Watteau

1710

1720

1720

Polish lady, after Watteau   English gentleman   French girl, after Watteau

1720

1715

1717

English woman   after Watteau   Two French gentlemen

1720

1725

Boy

Girl

Details after Watteau

Riding gaiters

Wig

1725

1724

Cuff

French lady

Dutch gentleman

French lady

after Watteau

German gentleman

Noble lady

Gentlemen of the early eighteenth century

Culotte   Gaiters   Postillion boot

French woman, after Chardin

French gentleman

English lady, after Hogarth

English lady

English gentleman

French lady

Four French gentlemen

Historical Survey

MIDDLE EIGHTEENTH CENTURY (1745-1765)

1748: End of the War of the Austrian Succession.

1749: *Tom Jones,* by Henry Fielding (1707-54).

1754: Beginning of the French and Indian Wars, the American phase of the Seven Years' War, with Great Britain and the Colonies aligned against the French and Indians.

1755: *A Dictionary of the English Language,* by Samuel Johnson (1709-84).

1756: Start of the Seven Years' War in Europe:

Prussia and England against Austria and France.

1759: *Candide,* by Voltaire (1694-1778).

1760: Beginning of reign of George III of England (1728-1820).

c. 1760: "Death of General Wolfe," by Benjamin West (1738-1820), American painter.

1762: *Orfeo ed Euridice,* by Christoph Gluck (1714-87), German composer.

1763: The Treaty of Paris ended the Seven Years' War.

French boy

Upper-class Venetians

French girl

French lady

Dandy, after Hogarth

English lady

French gentleman

Austrian woman

English gentleman

French gentleman

English county cavort

More English dancers

Four Hogarthians

Wig   Wig   Wig

Corset   Side hoops   Ladies' shoes

French girl

English county squirearchy

Three English gentlemen

French street types

German

Venetian wig and mask

Periwig

after van Loo

after Boucher

Venetian

Hogarth self-portrait

German

after Nattier

Men's gloves

after Gainsborough

Women's gloves

Historical Survey

LATE EIGHTEENTH CENTURY (1765-1800)

1765: Stamp Act passed by parliament; nine colonies protested against "taxation without representation."

East India Company given joint territorial sovereignty, with the crown, over India.

1769: Mme. Du Barry became virtual ruler of the French court, through her influence over Louis XV.

Steam engine patented by James Watt (1736-1819), Scottish inventor and engineer.

1770: Spinning jenny patented by James Hargreaves, English inventor.

c. 1770: "Thomas Hancock," by John Singleton Copley (1738-1815), American portrait painter.

1774: Beginning of the reign of Louis XVI of France.

1775: War of American Independence; Continental Army led by George Washington (1732-99).

1776: Declaration of American Independence.

Volume I of *History of the Decline and Fall of the Roman Empire,* by Edward Gibbon (1737-94).

1777: Marquis de Lafayette (1757-1834) commissioned major general in Continental Army.

1778: Benjamin Franklin (1706-90) sent as American plenipotentiary to France.

1781: *Critique of Pure Reason,* by Immanuel Kant (1724-1804), German philosopher.

Bust, "Voltaire," by Jean Antoine Houdon (1741-1828), French sculptor.

1783: Treaty signed by Great Britain and the United States, ending the Revolution.

1784: "The Tragic Muse" (Mrs. Siddons), by Sir Joshua Reynolds (1723-92), English portrait painter.

1787: *Don Giovanni,* opera by Wolfgang Amadeus Mozart (1756-91).

1789: Fall of the Bastille; beginning of the French Revolution.

1791: *The Life of Samuel Johnson,* by James Boswell (1740-95).

1791-92: *The Rights of Man,* by Thomas Paine (1737-1809).

1791-95: "London" symphonies, by Joseph Haydn (1732-1809).

1792: French First Republic established.

1793: Louis XVI guillotined; Reign of Terror began. It ended with the fall of Robespierre in 1794.

1794: *Songs of Experience,* by William Blake (1757-1827).

1794 ff.: Portraits of George Washington by Gilbert Stuart (1755-1828), American portrait painter.

1795: Directory established in France.

1797: "Kubla Khan," by Samuel Taylor Coleridge (1772-1834).

1798: Napoleon Bonaparte (1769-1821) began his Egyptian campaign.

1799: The Consulate established in France, with Napoleon as First Consul.

"Sabine Women," by Jacques Louis David (1748-1825), French classical painter.

French lady

English gentlemen

English boy

Upper-class English couple

English boy

People of the English squirearchy

1765

1765

Periwigs

1760

1765

English squire

Man's shirt

Coat vent

1765

Back details

Bodice

English lady

Middle-class Germans

French lady

English actress

French noble

English lady

Four Frenchmen

English girl

French lady

English sport

Figures in French court life

Four men of the French court

1771

1770

1775

Coat vent decoration   **Cocked hat**   Italian corset   Woman's shoe   Umbrella

1778

1782

1779

1780

Hoops

English sports

English gentleman

1785

English sports

English lady

English gentleman

1780

Marie Antoinette

1785

c. 1785

1785

1780

English gentlemen

Boot garter   Breeches   Classic drape   Collar, scarf, and vest detail

Fashionable French women

Boulevard figures

Fashionable dress

Girl and admirer

Young lady

Duchess of Chinchón

Duchess of Alba

Marquesa de las Mercedes

Duchess of Alba

Carlos III

Carlos IV

Duke de Fernán Nuñez

Son of the artist

FRENCHMAN OF THE SECOND EMPIRE, AFTER DISDERI

The Nineteenth Century

THE OPENING years of the nineteenth century were marked by a very radical change in style of dress — a reversion to the classical simplicity of Greece and Rome. This revival had had its inception during the Directoire (1795-1799), partly under the impetus of the painter David, and was encouraged by Napoleon during the Empire period.

In the field of women's clothing, corsets were abandoned and the outer gown became a simple white muslin sheath girdled just under the bosom and allowed to fall straight to the ground. The Grecian effect was completed by a low square neckline, short puffed sleeves, white clocked stockings, pumps with low heels, and hair styles similar to those of classic times. Tremendous scoop bonnets were worn, and long gloves reached to the upper arm. The spencer, a short, close-fitting jacket, soon came into style, and cashmere shawls were popular.

Toward the end of the '20s there was another quite radical reversal in fashions as women shifted back toward romanticism. The skirt was belled out by undergarments, the shortened sleeve increased in bulk, and hair was curled, producing a "butterfly" appearance. The simple, tubular gown disappeared for a century, and bows, ribbons, and feminine furbelows became high style. Fabric, too, changed from simple muslins to pastel-colored stiff materials.

In the middle '50s, at the time of Napoleon III, crinoline was introduced: a material made of horsehair and linen, shaped and wired so as to extend the skirt even more than had been stylish in the '40s. For the '50s and '60s we may take as the prototype of femininity the picture of the Countess of Castiglione, which we have reproduced. Her immense flowing skirt, tiny waist, and nude shoulders are features of a style that was both constrictive and artificial. The most popular headgear was the small hat, tipped forward, introduced by the Empress Eugénie.

During this period there was marked differentiation in types of clothing, each time of day and each occupation necessitating a complete change of dress. The first separate blouse and skirt combination — that boon to women for the past hundred years — was introduced. The fabrics associated with the period were the same stiff-textured cloth of the earlier decade, with cottons for summer wear. Daytime colors were brown, rust, gray, and green, as well as Scottish plaids; pale pastels were used for evening dresses. Lace mitts, parasols, and pouch bags with wooden handles were carried by every woman of fashion. The hair was worn neatly parted and drawn back into a snood; snoods were also worn during the evening, but in this case they were ornamented.

During the '60s and '70s the extreme circular hooped skirt was abandoned, partly in response to new modes of travel: trains, boats, and trams. The full skirts were pulled to the rear and supported by a sort of wire cage, which by 1876 was about a foot in depth — the antecedent of the bustle of the '80s. Though corsets were somewhat looser, the bust continued to be accentuated. Style innovations included the high collar and long, tight sleeve, full at the top, which would later become the leg-o'-mutton sleeve. Lace jabots and edgings were used at the neck.

Travel to resorts and spas of Europe resulted in the development of more simple and practical clothing; and the trend toward country life, with its attendant upper-class sports, gave rise to a further need for variety and practicality. Among the general populace, "Sunday-go-to-meeting" clothes were in marked contrast to the weekday work clothes; in many regions the traditional peasant garments were rapidly outmoded by the spread of industry.

Men's styles changed much less than women's during the century. In general there were only tiny and subtle refinements in the tailoring of the suit introduced during the eighteenth century; and even these changes were made only by men of fashion and wealth. The clothing of Napoleon, as representative of the early classical revival, consisted of tight elasticized breeches of buff-colored wool, colorful waistcoat, frock coat of brown broadcloth with a high stand-up collar, white stockings, and pointed, heelless shoes similar to modern patent-leather pumps. The male dandy, the *incroyable,* carried these styles to extremes, affecting the casual, free look of prominent patriots of the day. He wore a large, unfitted coat with clawhammer tails, high-collared coat and shirt, and a silk cravat wrapped several times around the neck, all of which gave the figure a top-heavy look. His hairdress, too, affected the unkempt appearance of the revolutionist. In contrast to this *avant-garde* group, the French gentlemen of the day adopted the English suit, which had first appeared as a hunting costume, and converted it to daytime and evening wear.

At a later period styles became somewhat effeminate. Long buff, striped, and checked trousers slimmed down to the ankle and strapped under the instep. The tailed frock coat pinched in tightly at the waist and curved out at the chest and hips, creating a feminine outline. The coat opened in front to reveal a frilly expanse of shirting, and a black silk scarf tied around a stand-up collar. Hair was softly curled, and beards and sideburns came into fashion.

In general, long, tight trousers, knee-length frock coat, mustaches and beards remained fashionable. By 1870 a man of fashion would include in his wardrobe the following items: a velvet-collared Chesterfield for dress wear, a light-colored short sack coat, a riding outfit, coats to be worn with odd checked and striped trousers, distinct evening clothes very like our present formal dress, an early type of dinner coat, linen sack suits, an Inverness cape, broad four-in-hand ties as well as bow ties and wrapped cravats, a Homburg hat, bowler, boating hat, woolen visored caps, and small cricket cap.[1]

1. Acknowledgment is made to Dr. Cecil Willett Cunnington, author of *English Women's Clothing of the Nineteenth Century,* and to Faber and Faber Ltd., London, for the sketches initialed CWC in the pages following, adapted from drawings in that book.

Historical Survey

1804: First Empire established in France, with Napoleon as emperor.

1805: Nelson defeated the French at Trafalgar. "Madame Rivière," by Jean Auguste Ingres (1780-1867), French classical painter.

1805-06: *The Prelude*, by William Wordsworth (1770-1850).

1806: Holy Roman Empire came to an end when Francis II, Emperor of Austria, dropped the title of Holy Roman Emperor.

1808: Part 1 of *Faust*, by Johann Wolfgang von Goethe (1749-1832).

1810-13: "Disasters of War," by Goya (1746-1828), Spanish painter, etcher, and lithographer.

1811: Regency established in England, with Prince of Wales (later George IV) regent for George III.

1812: Napoleon invaded Russia; retreated with terrific losses.

1813: *Pride and Prejudice*, by Jane Austen (1775-1817).

1814: Napoleon abdicated, was sent to Elba; Louis XVIII placed on the throne. In 1815 Napoleon left Elba, entered Paris, was defeated decisively by Wellington at Waterloo, abdicated a second time, and was sent to St. Helena, where he died in 1821.

1814-15: Congress of Vienna, dominated by Metternich (1773-1859), chancellor of Austria.

1815: French monarchy re-established, with Louis XVIII as king.

1816: *Barber of Seville*, opera by Gioacchino Rossini (1792-1868).

1818: George Gordon, Lord Byron (1788-1824), English poet, started *Don Juan*.

1819: *The World, as Will and Idea*, by Arthur Schopenhauer (1788-1860), German philosopher.

Ivanhoe, by Sir Walter Scott (1771-1832).

"Ode to the West Wind," by Percy Bysshe Shelley (1792-1822).

"Raft of the Medusa," by Jean Louis Géricault (1791-1824), French romantic painter.

1820: "Ode on a Grecian Urn," by John Keats (1795-1821).

1823: *Ninth Symphony*, by Ludwig van Beethoven (1770-1827).

1824: "Massacre of Scio," by Ferdinand Victor Eugène Delacroix (1799-1863), French romantic painter.

1827-28: "Winterreise" song cycle by Franz Schubert (1797-1828).

c. 1830: "Honfleur, Houses on the Quay," by Jean Baptiste Corot (1796-1875), French landscape painter.

1831: *Le Rouge et le noir*, by Stendhal (1783-1842).

1832: The first Reform Bill, in England, restored the democratic character of the British parliament and extended the franchise.

1835: First series of *Fairy Tales*, by Hans Christian Andersen (1805-75).

1835-40: *Democracy in America*, by Alexis de Tocqueville (1805-59).

1837: Victoria (1819-1901) became Queen of England.

The French Revolution by Thomas Carlyle (1795-1881).

1839: The invention of the daguerreotype was announced by Louis Daguerre (1789-1851), French painter and inventor.

c. 1839: *Opus 28* (24 Preludes), by Frédéric Chopin (1810-49).

1840: "Dichterliebe" and "Frauenliebe und -Leben" song cycles by Robert Schumann (1810-56).

1842: First series of *La Comédie humaine*, by Honoré de Balzac (1799-1850), French novelist.

Music for Shakespeare's *Midsummer Night's*

Dream completed by Felix Mendelssohn (1809-47), German composer and pianist.

1843: *A System of Logic,* by John Stuart Mill (1806-73), English philosopher and economist.

1844: "Rain, Steam and Speed," by Joseph William Turner (1775-1851), English painter.

1844-55: *Experimental Researches in Electricity,* by Michael Faraday (1791-1867), English chemist and physicist.

These figures after Ingres

1806

1807

1803

Two French ladies

German lady

1810

1803

1806

1805

French dandy

English prizefighter

Full dress

English groom

1807

1800

1801

1809

Hairdos and hats, 1800-10

1801

1801

1810

Spencer   Shoes   Muslin chemisette

French ladies

Four French gentlemen

1812
1815
1815

Women's shoes

Spencers

c. 1818

Fashionable French ladies

c. 1815

1816

Three French ladies

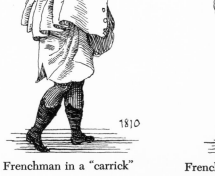

1811

Frenchman

English sport

1810

Frenchman in a "carrick"

Frenchman in a riding coat

German gentleman

Goethe

French boulevardier

French gentleman, after Ingres

George IV

after a French fashion plate

Two upper-class Englishmen

French gentleman

Count d'Orsay

Styles in hats, 1820-30

1823

1824

Four French ladies, after Geszler

1830

1822

Two French ladies

French lady, after Ingres

Four fashionable French ladies

141

Women's shoes

Bodice, front and back

c. 1838

Fashion of the late '30s

Count d'Orsay

1831

French lady of fashion

1832

1837

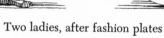

Two ladies, after fashion plates

1830

French lady

1832

Russian gentlemen

1839

German and Italian gentlemen

French gentleman

143

Historical Survey

MIDDLE NINETEENTH CENTURY (1845-1865)

1846: *The Damnation of Faust,* by Hector Berlioz (1803-69), French composer.

1847: *Jane Eyre,* by Charlotte Brontë (1816-55).

1847-48: *Vanity Fair,* by William Makepeace Thackeray (1811-63).

1848: Revolution in France, formation of Second Republic, Louis Napoleon, president. *Wuthering Heights,* by Emily Brontë (1818-48).

1849: "The Funeral at Ornans," by Gustave Courbet (1819-77), French realistic painter.

1852: Second Empire established in France, with Louis Napoleon (1808-73) emperor, as Napoleon III.

1854-56: Crimean War: Russia against Turkey, England, France, and Sardinia.

1857: *Madame Bovary,* by Gustave Flaubert (1821-80), French novelist.

Les Fleurs du mal, by Charles Baudelaire (1821-67), French poet.

1858: East India Company dissolved; government of India transferred to the British crown.

1859: *On the Origin of Species . . . ,* by Charles Darwin (1809-82).

A Tale of Two Cities, by Charles Dickens (1812-70).

First *Idylls of the King,* by Alfred, Lord Tennyson (1809-92).

1862: *Les Misérables,* by Victor Hugo (1802-85).

c. 1863: "Washwoman," by Honoré Daumier (1808-79), French caricaturist.

1864: Archduke Maximilian of Austria sent to Mexico by Napoleon III as emperor. Juárez forced his surrender in 1867, and Maximilian was court-martialed and shot.

Middle-class fashions

1845

1840

1845

Three fashionable ladies, after Winterhalter

c. 1845

c. 1845

1840

Gentleman wearing a paletot

Three French gentlemen

1844

1845 1849

1841 1844

c. 1845

1849

Women's shoes

Corset and muff

c. 1850

Middle-class French people

1859

c. 1850

c. 1850

French lady, after Disderi

English-Scottish ladies and gentleman

1850

1852

François Pierre Guizot

Frenchman

Adèle Hugo

Frenchman

147

English woman

German gentleman

American lady

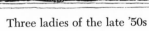

Three ladies of the late '50s

Four gentlemen

Three upper-class French people

French lady

Two middle-class Frenchmen

French lady

Lord Palmerston

Coignet

Frenchman

Criori père

149

Muslin fichu

Day sleeve

1855

Morning sleeve

c. 1855

1852

1851

Ladies, after Ingres

Jacket

1853

Lace bertha

c.1858

Upper-class Austrians

c.1858

c.1860

Austrian gentleman and lady

French lady

c.1858

English lady

Three well-bred Austrians

151

Three French gentlemen

Princess Clotilde

Prince Jerome Bonaparte

Madame de Gerantin

Four fashionable men

Baron de Talleyrand

MacQuard

General Bosco

Scottish lady, after Hill

Countess de Castiglione

German lady

1858

1859

From the artist's photograph collection

Historical Survey

1865: Gregor Mendel (1822-84), Austrian botanist, first published his Laws of heredity.
History of English Literature, by Hippolyte Taine (1828-93), French philosopher and critic.
Alice's Adventures in Wonderland, by Charles Dodgson (Lewis Carroll, 1832-98).

1866: *War and Peace,* by Count Leo Tolstoi (1828-1910).
La Vie Parisienne, by Jacques Offenbach (1819-80), German-born French composer.

1867: Reform Bill redistributed parliamentary seats and extended the suffrage in England.
Volume I of *Das Kapital,* by Karl Marx (1818-83).

1869: Opening of the Suez Canal.
The Ring and the Book completed by Robert Browning (1812-89).

c. 1870: Beginning of the Impressionist movement in painting; among its most noted participants were Édouard Manet (1832-83), Claude Monet (1840-1926), Edgar Degas 1834-1917), Pierre Auguste Renoir (1841-1919), and Camille Pissarro (1830-1903).

1870-71: Franco-Prussian War, ending with the loss of Alsace-Lorraine to Germany, led to the formation of the German Empire and the French Third Republic.

1871: Bismarck (1815-98), Prussian statesman, became first chancellor of the new German Empire.
Paris Commune, modeled on communalistic principles, set up in Paris by insurrectionary government.
Aïda, opera by Giuseppe Verdi (1813-1901).

1874: First performance of *Boris Godunov,* by Modest Musorgski (1835-81), Russian composer.

1875: Under the aegis of Prime Minister Benjamin Disraeli (1804-81), Great Britain purchased an interest in the Suez Canal.

1876: "Afternoon of a Faun," by Stéphane Mallarmé (1842-98), French symbolic poet. The *Ring* cycle of Richard Wagner (1813-83) played at the opening of his Bayreuth Theater.

1880: *The Brothers Karamazov,* by Fëdor Dostoevski (1821-81), Russian novelist.

1883 ff.: *Thus Spake Zarathustra,* by Friedrich Nietzsche (1844-1900), German philosopher and poet.

1886: *Fourth Symphony* of Johannes Brahms (1833-97).

1887: Gottlieb Daimler (1834-1900), German engineer and inventor, patented a high-speed internal-combustion machine.

1888: *Fifth Symphony,* by Pëtr Ilich Tchaikovsky (1840-93), Russian composer.

1890: *Hedda Gabler,* by Henrik Ibsen (1828-1906).

c. 1890: Post-impressionist movement in painting; most important in the group were Paul Cézanne (1839-1906), Vincent van Gogh (1853-90), Paul Gauguin (1848-1903), and Georges Seurat (1859-91).

1892: "At the Moulin Rouge," by Henri Toulouse-Lautrec (1864-1901), French painter.

1894: Alfred Dreyfus (1859-1935), French Army officer, convicted of treason by means of perjured evidence.

Jacques Offenbach

Napoleon III and his Empress

Prince of Wales

1862

French girl, after Monet

1868

French gentleman, after Manet

1866

French lady, after Monet

Russian ambassador

Scotsman

General Bruce

Englishman

1868

1868

1867

1860

1874

1850s

1868

1863

1869

1862

Ladies' shoes

Puffed horsehair crinoline

Wired crinoline

Habit shirt

English woman   Old farmer of Croft   English lady

Miss Jelf   B. Woodward, Esq.   Gardener

Lord Eniskillen   Captain Smith   The Reverend Smith   Attendant

1861

German ladies

Fashionable costumes of the sixties.

Fashionable male attire, after German fashion plates

English ladies

1862

German princess

1862

Lord Chesterfield

Well-born German couple

Count Bela Széchény

Four ladies

Three English ladies of fashion

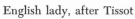

English lady, after Tissot

French gentleman, after Manet

French lady, after Renoir

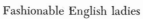

Fashionable English ladies

Three women, after Manet

1876

English lady

Sarah Bernhardt

1874

French lady

1870

English lady

1878

French actress

1873

English lady

Gentlemen of fashion

163

Three fashionable ladies

Three ladies, after contemporary fashion plates

Four gentlemen, after German fashion plates

1885

1880

1881

1882

Women's shoes

1888

1888

1887

Bustle

Bust improver

Two English ladies

French barmaid

English lady

Fashionable English costume

English lady   Jane Hading   Austrian lady   Lady Dunlo (May Bilton)

EDWARDIAN ENGLISHMAN

The Turn of the Century

A S THE century drew to an end, France continued to be the fashion center of the woman's world. Toulouse-Lautrec's pictures show us the clothing of the Parisian demimonde of this era; and Renoir's, that of the Parisian middle class.

By 1890 the bustle had disappeared, though hips were still prominent. Women's waists continued to be tightly constricted; the bosom in front and the hips behind were accentuated, resulting in a very curious and unnatural hourglass shape. The leg-o'-mutton sleeve became overexaggerated as it grew popular. Tailored suits were very much the rage, especially in England, where country life had great influence on fashion. Sports, into which women entered more and more, also became important factors in determining styles. As women's spheres of activity broadened, the shirtwaist and the tailored separate skirt became both fashionable and usual. In contrast to the rather severe outer daytime clothes, very dainty underwear was worn, and lace frills appeared at wrist and throat and clustered over negligées and tea gowns. Corsets continued their unquestioned reign; women were not yet prepared to surrender this greatest emblem of bondage to conventionality.

Small hats, set on top of the head, were decorated with the plumage of exotic birds. The hair was long and worn high, with waves frothing around the forehead.

During the period 1900-1910 the outline was revised as an up-and-down corseted whole. Trains were usual, even with suits, until about 1910, when skirts began to rise. At that time women's fashions reverted to the styles of the Napoleon I era as waists became higher and dresses longer. The hobble skirt and the slit skirt made their appearance. High-buttoned shoes are associated with this period, together with ridiculously large and ornate hats.

As World War I approached, women returned to a quite normal silhouette. The "harem" skirt, here illustrated, seems to be a precursor of present-day slacks. In general skirts became shorter, about eight inches off the ground, and began to flare out. Hats were lower and wider, producing the strange effect we have illustrated.

In America World War I introduced new freedoms for women and released them from the rigidities of nineteenth-century traditions, in clothing as well as in more significant spheres. Europe lost its pre-eminence as style arbiter, therefore the changes that took place after 1918 are discussed here only in relation to the American scene.

Historical Survey

TURN OF THE CENTURY (1895-1914)

1895: *The Importance of Being Earnest,* by Oscar Wilde (1856-1900).
The Time Machine, by H. G. Wells (1866-1946).
Jude the Obscure, by Thomas Hardy (1840-1928).

1896: *La Bohème,* opera by Giacomo Puccini (1858-1924).

1897: Diamond Jubilee of Queen Victoria.

1897 ff.: *Studies in the Psychology of Sex,* by Havelock Ellis (1859-1939).

1899-1902: The Boer War, ending with the loss of independence by the Boer republics.

1900: *The Interpretation of Dreams,* by Sigmund Freud (1856-1939).
Lord Jim, by Joseph Conrad (1857-1924).

1902: *Pelléas et Mélisande,* by Claude Debussy (1862-1918), French composer.

1903: *Man and Superman,* by George Bernard Shaw (1856-1950).

1904: The Abbey Theatre established; William Butler Yeats (1865-1939), Irish poet and dramatist, important in its development.

c. 1905: "Les Fauves" first exhibited as a group. Chief representatives of this movement were the French painters Henri Matisse (1869- ——), Georges Rouault (1871- ——), André Derain (1880- ——), Raoul Dufy (1878- ——), and Georges Braque (1881- ——).

1907: *Strait Is the Gate,* by André Gide (1869-1951).
"Les Demoiselles d'Avignon," by Pablo Picasso (1881- ——), Spanish painter and sculptor.

1908: *The Song of the Earth,* by Gustav Mahler (1860-1911), Bohemian composer.

1910: Death of Edward VII, King of England.

1911: South Pole discovered by Roald Amundsen (1872-1928), Norwegian explorer.

1912: *Daphnis and Chloë* ballet suite, by Maurice Ravel (1875-1937).

c. 1912: "Composition Number 4," by Vasili Kandinski (1866-1944), Russian painter and designer.

1913: *Swann's Way*, by Marcel Proust (1871-1922).

Sons and Lovers, by D. H. Lawrence (1885-1930).

Le Sacre du printemps ballet, by Igor Stravinsky (1882-——), Russian composer.

1914: Beginning of World War I.

Dubliners, by James Joyce (1882-1941).

Adjustable train

1898

Bustle

Tucked shirtwaist

Woolen knickers

Corset

1893

Ladies' shoes

M. Boileau

The Englishman (and others) at the Moulin Rouge

Georges-Henri Manuel

La Goulue

Henry Nocq

Deaf Bertha

Honorine P.

Two models

Three ladies

1895

1898

German lady

Models

Gentlemen's clothing, after German fashion plates

English lady

Richard Mansfield

Contemporary bathing dress

Four ladies, with Rudyard Kipling

Edward Terry

English lady

Fashionable mourning

French model

175

Fashionable dress, from *Vogue*

1912

1914

1910

Three French models

Two English gentlemen

French model

The harem skirt

1919

1917

1919

Three upper-class English people

c 1919

c.1919

Fashionable people, from *Vogue*

Part III
AMERICAN COSTUME

FARMERS, COOPERSTOWN, NEW YORK

Eastern America: 1840-1880

FROM the early seventeenth century until World War I Americans slavishly imitated fashions from abroad. I have started this section in 1840 since it was at that time that photography became an important art form, faithfully mirroring the customs of the day. In general, the American way of life prior to this time had brought about few changes in the essentially European styles.

During the trying years of the Civil War, Reconstruction, and industrial expansion we find that the predominant influence in men's clothing was the image of the statesman — men such as Clay, Webster, and Lincoln. Most men wished to look substantial, to impress their peers, to present a distinguished and lofty appearance. The lawyer-statesman, most ably exemplified by Lincoln, invariably wore a sober black suit, white linen, black scarf tie, a tall silk hat, and boots which were soon to become congress gaiters. It was impressive clothing for the orator's flourish, the lawyer's summation.

Work clothing included boots and a woolen double-breasted shirt, pullover in style — that is, opening only to the waist. The coat shirt, buttoning from top to bottom, was a later development.

In Boston in the '40s, as Southworth and Hawes showed in their remarkable daguerreotypes, men of substance added to the basic costume all possible traces of elegance. The old gentleman in the quilted coat is not unlike Guizot, the Frenchman, who is portrayed in the European section. Obviously he considers himself above the run of rural lawyers. Our "Boston Beauty," too, is super-refined for an American; it is easy to believe that she has made the Grand Tour with her cultivated parents. A group of women dressed in these fashions must have given a fine tone to the colonnaded porches of Saratoga in August.

The women of the era who accompanied their black-suited, ambitious husbands dressed according to the edicts from abroad, as interpreted in the East by *Godey's Lady's Book*. The all-pervasive conventionality of clothing in this period of civil conflict is astonishing; as witnessed by the oppressive constriction that is sensed in the picture of Mrs. Lincoln on page 189.

Historical Survey

1787 TO 1880

1787: Constitution of the United States was adopted.

1789: George Washington (1732-99) inaugurated first President.

1794: Cotton gin patented by Eli Whitney (1765-1825).

1803: Louisiana purchased from France by President Jefferson (1743-1826).

1804-1806: Lewis and Clark led expedition to discover a route to the Pacific Ocean.

1812-15: War of 1812.

1823: Monroe Doctrine, prohibiting further European expansion on American continent.

1825: Erie Canal completed.

1841: First *Essays* by Ralph Waldo Emerson (1803-82).
The Deerslayer, by James Fenimore Cooper (1789-1851).

1843: *The Gold Bug*, by Edgar Allan Poe (1809-49).

1844: First telegraph message sent by Samuel

F. B. Morse (1791-1872), inventor and portrait painter.

1845: "Fur Traders Descending the Missouri" painted by George Caleb Bingham (1811-79).

1846: Sewing machine patented by Elias Howe (1819-67).

1846-48: War with Mexico, ending with the ceding of large territories to the United States.

1848: Discovery of gold at Sutter's Mill in California, leading to the Gold Rush of '49. *Songs of the Sable Harmonists*, by Stephen C. Foster (1826-64).

1850: *The Scarlet Letter*, by Nathaniel Hawthorne (1804-64).

1851: *Moby-Dick*, by Herman Melville (1819-91).

1852: *Uncle Tom's Cabin*, by Harriet Beecher Stowe (1811-96).

1854: *Walden*, by Henry David Thoreau (1817-62).

1855: *Leaves of Grass,* by Walt Whitman (1819-92).

The Song of Hiawatha, by Henry Wadsworth Longfellow (1807-82).

1857: Dred Scott decision, denying citizenship to Negroes.

1859: John Brown, rabid abolitionist, raided Harper's Ferry arsenal to incite a slave revolt; convicted of treason and hanged the same year.

1860: Abraham Lincoln (1809-65) elected to the Presidency; South Carolina seceded from the Union.

1861: Other slave states seceded from the Union; beginning of the Civil War.

"Delaware Water Gap" painted by George Inness (1825-94).

1862: First Homestead Act, opening western lands to settlement.

1863: Lincoln's Emancipation Proclamation, freeing slaves in states in rebellion; Gettysburg address.

1865: Lincoln assassinated five days after the surrender of Robert E. Lee.

Thirteenth Amendment ratified, abolishing slavery.

1866: *Snow-Bound,* by John Greenleaf Whittier (1807-92).

1867: Alaska purchased from Russia.

1868: *Little Women,* by Louisa M. Alcott (1832-88).

1869: Completion of first transcontinental railroad route.

1872: "Portrait of My Mother" painted by James A. M. Whistler (1834-1903).

1875: *Science and Health,* by Mary Baker Eddy (1821-1910).

"The Surgical Clinic of Prof. Gross" painted by Thomas Eakins (1844-1916).

1876: Battle of the Little Big Horn, in which General George Custer, in charge of an Army expedition, was ambushed and killed by Sioux Indians led by Sitting Bull and Crazy Horse.

Telephone patented by Alexander Graham Bell (1847-1922).

1877: Phonograph patented by Thomas A. Edison (1847-1931).

F. Langenheim

Forty-niners prepared

Eastern gentleman

Boston beauty

Rev. W. Sampson

T. H. Benton

Henry Clay

Mathew Brady

Daniel Webster

Boy

Judge Lemuel Shaw

Charlotte Cushman

Matilde Hays

John Quincy Adams

Mrs. Vincent

Sam Houston

185

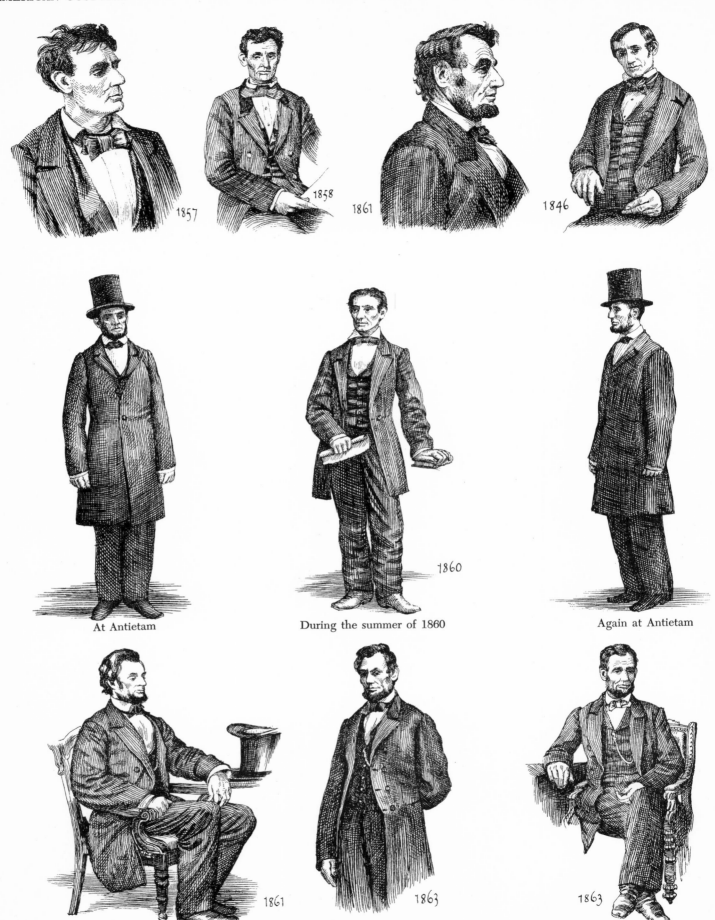

1857

1858

1861

1846

At Antietam

During the summer of 1860

1860

Again at Antietam

1861

1863

1863

Figures of Lincoln from Stefan Lorant's *Lincoln in Photographs*

Lady of the '60s

Member of the Oneida Community

Fashionable lady

Prosperous figures of the '60s

Young man

Three fashionable ladies

187

Allan Pinkerton

Mrs. George B. McClelland

Lincoln's murderer

Stephen A. Douglas

Three ladies

Middle-class New Yorkers

H. Hamlin

Andrew Johnson

W. H. Jackson

Gentleman, after Brady

Belle Boyd

Pauline Cushman

Mrs. Lincoln

Jeremiah Black

William Wilkins

Clara Barton

Wendell Phillips

Fashionable ladies of the '60s

John Coburn   C. Ellsworth   C. A. Dana

c. 1869

Lady   E. M. Stanton   Ulysses S. Grant   Skating costume

President Hayes

Summer vacationer

Gentleman

Alice Motley

Charles E. and Ida Angle

Addie Motley

Four fashionable women of the '70s

Three fashionable ladies

Two fashionable ladies

Jennie Lee, actress

Gentleman

Jay Gould

Jim Fiske

Actor

Eastern America: 1880-1900

THE TWO Lebanon (New Hampshire) belles above are typical middle-class girls of the later '80s, at which time the wrap-around overskirt and the tight basque, or jacket, were considered right and proper. The frilled, tiered, gathered-behind skirt of the '70s was a thing of the past. The sashes and apron-like garments of that time were drawn back, producing the bustle characteristic of the period. Even the tennis player is similarly garbed, though one wonders how she played the game. Mr. Dakin's remarkable snapshots taken in Cherry Valley (New York) late in the '80s show us a whole party gaily jumping over a tennis net, indicating that these apparently crippling clothes actually permitted a good deal of motion. Several of Mr. Dakin's friends in Cherry Valley remind us of the Dutch costume of the mid-1600s. Women of that time also pulled their skirts up before and behind and wore very similar flat-brimmed, high-crowned hats.

Men usually wore a derby, which had originated earlier in the century, now sometimes gray or brown as well as the more usual black. They often affected "sportiness": gay blazers and cricket caps.

The sophistication in dress and the gracefulness of living found in a little hamlet like Cherry Valley are of much social interest. One is suddenly able to people those stately, rather ugly gingerbread mansions of rural America and to believe in the dignified conventionality which they once represented.

Following quickly on the heels of the tennis players are the young business-women of the '90s, photographed by Byron as they left the West Shore Ferry at Forty-second Street on their way to offices in the city. Their shirtwaists and bell skirts, though certainly ornate and unwieldy, are far simpler than the clothing of the '70s and '80s.

Among non-laboring classes of the '90s, sleeves became greatly puffed, bosoms ample and prominent, waists tiny, and skirts full and free-falling.

Men, with their straw hats and square suits, have a definitely modern appearance except for the high-buttoned coat, the top button of which was so close to the throat that the shirt collar was almost invisible. It was a common practice to wear a semi-cutaway coat with odd trousers. The semi-cutaway ended at the waist in front and slanted to semi-tails in the back. Shirt cuffs were frequently false, fitted into the coat sleeve like wrist bands. Both derbies and silk hats were always worn with their brims level. The oxford shoe had not yet made its appearance, and high-buttoned or high-laced shoes were universal. Fashionable accessories were heavy gold watch chains or black ribbon fobs with a gold-encased jewel.

Historical Survey

THE EIGHTIES AND NINETIES

1881: *The Portrait of a Lady,* by Henry James (1843-1916).

1884: "Life-Line" painted by Winslow Homer (1836-1910).
"Toilers of the Sea," by Albert Ryder (1847-1917), exhibited.

1885: *Adventures of Huckleberry Finn,* by Samuel L. Clemens (Mark Twain, 1835-1910).

1885-86: Geronimo (1829-1909), Apache chieftain, led uprising against the whites.

1886: Haymarket labor riot in Chicago.

1888: Kodak invented by George Eastman (1854-1932).

1894: Coxey's Army of unemployed marched on Washington.
First public showing of Edison's Kinetoscope.

1896: Klondike gold rush.

1898: Destruction of U.S.S. *Maine* in Havana harbor, led to Spanish-American War.

1899: *The Theory of the Leisure Class,* by Thorstein Veblen (1857-1929).

Three correct young ladies of Cherry Valley, N. Y.

A fine example of conspicuous leisure

Figures on this page courtesy of Mrs. Pauline Dakin Taft, Oberlin, Ohio

Three friends of the Dakins'

Two ladies and a gentleman of Cherry Valley, N. Y.

Figures on this page courtesy of Mrs. Pauline Dakin Taft, Oberlin, Ohio

Young ladies of the '80s

Tennis enthusiast   Correct street costume   Amateur photographer

George Eastman   Cherry Valley sports

Prize fight referee

1898

L. N. Kenton

1900

Professor Miller

1901

Miss Harrison

1881

J. M. Hamilton

1895

Weda Cook

1892

Mrs. L. W. J. Bacon

1888

Professor Rowland

1891

1903

Thomas Eakins, from a photogra

1866

Three ladies, after Byron

Lady shopper

Wedding guest

Lady strolling

Street types of the city, after E. A. Austin

Three girls at Coney Island

Coney Island trippers

Three New York ladies

Street hawker

Mrs. M. K. Wetmore

Miss Frances Griscom

Young lady

Nellie Bly

Girls dancing

Lady, after Sargent

Howe and Hummell

W. J. Travis

William H. Crane

Newsman

Central Park skaters

Gentleman

Office girls leaving the West 42nd Street Ferry

Central Park boater

Young gentleman

Sarah, Rube, and Ann Warner

Calvin Coolidge

FUR TRAPPER

The American Frontier:
Across the Plains

AMERICAN, English, and French trappers, traders, and voyageurs were the first to penetrate the wilderness reaches of the West. They dressed somewhat as you see them here. The artist Alfred Jacob Miller, reproductions of whose work may be seen in Bernard De Voto's *Across the Wide Missouri*, pictures in his on-the-scene sketches of the '30s, the fashion of decorated Indian-style buckskin coats worn by Tom Tobin and Carson's grandson. Presumably these were for state occasions: contacts with the Indians, rendezvous, and the like. The trapping outfit was the plainer buckskin tunic with long fringes. The fringes of the early days were much longer than is commonly thought; it is said that they tended to drain off rain, and they were also a ready source of binding-thongs. Moccasins were the standard footwear; these were made by squaws, since the early trappers lived freely among the Indians. Old Jim Baker wears a wide-brimmed beaver hat, though caps of fur and felt were also common. Jim Bridger, who survived into the "settled" period of the Indian Wars, continued to live in the Indian style. General Arny is seen in another authentic Mountain Man outfit. Möllhausen was a German scientist who accompanied several expeditions to the West. I have included Remington's costume drawings on the assumption that they are authentic, as seems probable. The pictures of General Jack Casement, Union Pacific rail layer, and Harry Yount, Yellowstone Park Ranger, illustrate the more practical, more modern adaptations of these garments, as worn by "advance enterprisers."

By 1869 the lumbering industry had reached as far west as Michigan. The lumberjacks illustrated here were of this early period, and their clothing still shows pronounced French-Canadian influences. Lumbermen usually wore heavy fur coats and caps, the familiar plaid woolen shirts, and greased leather boots. An interesting French-Indian holdover was the Indian-designed sash frequently worn instead of a leather belt. The visored woolen cap with tied flaps which could be lowered over the ears was common in rural areas. A recent derivative of this cap is the more streamlined model worn by deer hunters.

Throughout the history of the frontier it will be noted that pioneers often continued to wear the type of clothing in which they had left the East. As was mentioned in an earlier section, Honest Abe Lincoln conformed to the ideal of the era — in clothing, as in most other respects. His style of dress was copied faithfully in border regions by frontiersmen, and even the glamorous cowboy donned a black suit and stiff white shirt when he went off the range into town. Though there were brief intervals in which frontiersmen adopted practical, useful garments adapted to some special purpose, such impulses were short-lived. The businessman's world, represented by the East, continued to be the model toward which each person tried to orient himself.

Bill Burrows

c.1830s

French traders or voyageurs

Tom Tobin, friend of Kit Carson's

Carson's grandson in original buckskin outfit

after Remington

after Alfred J. Miller

Antoine Clement

Joseph Meek

Old Jim Baker in beaver hat

W. H. Jackson

Miner

c. 1852

Prospector

Wells Fargo agent

General Arny

J. E. Johnson, stager

c. 1860

John McLoughlin

c. 1845

Mollhausen

1854

Andy Jackson

1845

A. T. Stewart

1856

Indian traders

Prospectors

D. O. Mills

Lewis A. Maverick

Miners

J. Bratt, tie-supplier to the Union Pacific

Agent

Cook at stage station

W. A. Gillespie, stage agent

Wild Bill Hickok

"Bishop" West, stager

General Jack Casement

Enoch Cummings, stager

Jim Bridger

Buffalo Bill

c.1866

Lumberjacks working, Michigan

c.1866

More early lumberjacks, Michigan

c.1890s

c.1875

'Jacks of a somewhat later period

211

James B. Gillett, ranger

T. J. McCoy

J. Clum, New Mexico Indian age

Fred W. Loring, correspondent

Prospector

Mickey Free

Members of a survey party, photographed by W. H. Jackson

Plains Characters

MANY of these examples of frontier clothing are taken from photographs made by William Henry Jackson, who did so much camera work in the West during the '70s and '80s. Here we see miners, stage drivers, marshals, scouts, "bad men," interpreters, and the like. These pictures illustrate the point already made — that apart from the cowboy's outfit there was little, if any, attempt to adapt clothing to the requirements of the job or to the environment. Men in the most remote, dangerous, and wild country wore the clerk's suit of the East, complete with fedora, starched shirt, and even a Prince Albert. However, some old hands, men like Bridger and Yount, made the practical shift to quasi-Indian buckskin and the sombrero, which would soon become the ubiquitous Stetson.

The most common type of work shirt, as in the East, was a woolen pullover. Boots were universally worn; usually they reached to just below the knees. The "Hollywood boot" — low, embossed, decorated, and bejeweled — was of course unknown and would have seemed ludicrous to pioneers. As long as the frontier was a region of hard work and danger there was no self-conscious posturing.

Many of the noted "bad men" were simply unemployed cowpunchers who descended to outlawry during hard times and in regions lacking adequate legal supervision. The outstanding plains characters were perhaps the most press-agented group in early American history. Billy the Kid and his colleagues were in no sense romantic, nor was their clothing at all splendid. Billy was essentially a driven, pathetic outcast, just as Calamity Jane was simply a drunkard who had talent for the dramatic. Buffalo Bill and Wild Bill Hickok were neither as good nor as bad as legend would lead one to believe. I have not included here a picture of Buffalo Bill's costume, since it was purely theatrical and was only distantly related to the clothes worn by men who were actually engaged in developing the frontier. A direct descendant of this type of fake Westernism is seen today in the Hopalong Cassidy costume. Certainly it bears little relation to fact, as can be seen by comparison with the cowboy section. I have included Pearl Hart here because her costume is authentic, though she was in fact an Easterner who had become bemused by the Western "bad man" legends.

The type of clothing actually worn by men during the early days of settlement is seen in the group called "Black Hills Pioneers, 1874." These are the men who broke the truce agreed upon by the U. S. Army and Red Cloud's Sioux Indians. Except for their aura of enterprising pioneer, they might have been seen in any western New York courthouse square on a Saturday night.

What amounted to a kind of "border" uniform was achieved by the Texas ranger pictured several times. His practical, neat outfit of boots, trousers, frontier shirt, vest, and Stetson admirably suited his calling. Captain John Hughes wears a Mexican sombrero, which, like the Stetson, is said to have been imported from good old Philadelphia. William "Flopping Bill" Cantrell and Sheriff Frank Canton are shown in a common winter outfit somewhat more comely than the range coat of buffalo skin.

Historical Survey

1845: Annexation of Texas; large areas of range given to cattle raisers. By 1860 there were over three million cattle in Texas; these were sold either locally or in New Orleans.

1865: Union stockyards in Chicago opened, but Chicago processed only Eastern-raised beef.

1866-68: The Missouri Pacific Railroad reached Kansas City and eventually Abilene. Thereafter cattle were driven north from Texas, over the Chisholm Trail, to processing centers. Boom towns quickly grew up around the railheads, but there was plenty of free open range to accommodate herds awaiting shipment.

1870: The bonanza ranching period began. Settlement of the Mormons in Utah and the growth of the Far West (initiated by discovery of gold and silver) provided ready Western markets. This was the golden age of the cowboy, since only he could adequately supervise the vast herds.

1879: Introduction of corn planters, binders, and other agricultural inventions opened the way to large-scale ranching and farming.

1886-87: Depression in the cattle business, caused by overcrowding, inexperience of cattle operators, disastrous winters, and Texas fever which afflicted the cattle.

1890 ff.: The old free range disappeared, and ranching became an organized, fenced-in operation. Homesteaders overflowed the land, and sheep were introduced. With these changes, the cowboy of legend also disappeared.

Biggs Davis

Dallas Studenmire

Westerner

Bass Outlaw

Black Bart

Billy the Kid

Jim Miller, stager

Deadwood sport

Frank James

Mike Tovey

Muleskinner

Hunter

Surveyor

Scout Billy McCabe

Calamity Jane

Judge John Fairchild

Westerner

Jack Crawford

O. C. Applegate

Frank Grouard

Black Hills prospectors

Rancher

Donald McKy, Indian scout

Sam Bass

Ranger

Charles N. Emery

John Nelson

Early Ku Klux Klansman

Teddy Blue

Scout C. S. Stobie, Calamity Jane, and Jack Crawford

John Burke

W. H. Jackson

H. Yount, Yellowstone Park ranger

Wild Bill (?)

Frank Riddle

Yellowstone Kelly

Surveyor

Josephine Meeker

Types of Nebraska settlers

Costumes worn by sod-house settlers

Four Nebraska settlers

Captain   Stevedores

Waiter in saloon   Captain Ben Howard and officers of the *City of Monroe*   Clerk

Steward and two friends

Pocatello land-rush policeman

Pullman strike cop

Pocatello land-rush policeman

Disturbed agrarians in Coxey's Army

Some of Coxey's marchers

Relatives and friends of the family

O. C. Damron

One of the Hatfields

T. F. Hunt, the photographer

Tom Chaffin

Devil Anse

Friend

W. E. Borden

Winter outfit

Harvey Logan and girl

John V. Farwell, rancher

Ranger

Stage guards

Walter Durbin, ranger

Deadwood citizen

Retired stager

Ranger

Captain John Hughes

Four young women down to hardpan

Two Klondike prospectors and a visiting actress

Three old-timers and a greenhorn

Actresses fording a stream in the Yukon

Three hopeful sourdoughs

New Hampshire lumberman   T. J. Butcher, Gates, Nebr.   F. Conley, of Nebraska   Sheriff Red Angus, Wyoming

COWBOY

The Cowboy

THE TRUE cowboy descended from the Spanish-Mexican vaquero, who, as Struthers Burt has pointed out, was in turn descended from the European Moors. The modern "Hollywood cowboy" is related to Buffalo Bill and the Wild West Shows rather than to the real cowpuncher. Today even the Texas ranger has been perverted by these influences, and the work clothing of the period 1870-1890, as here pictured and described, is gone forever.[1]

"Town" suits were usually dark woolens of conventional Eastern style. At work, cowboys sometimes wore canvas (duck) or leather jackets similarly cut. Working garb also included denim riding jackets, sometimes with corduroy collars. Suspenders and belts were rather rare, but occasionally a sash, like Charlie Russell's, was used. According to the Levi Strauss Company, the levis that appeared in Texas in the '50s, certainly by the '60s, were originally brown or natural canvas color; later they became blue. Copper-riveted levis were introduced in 1872-1873, but cowboys considered them a low-caste innovation and did not adopt them until the '90s. Vests were very common; they were convenient, and perhaps they also served as a link between the

1. Several of the details in this section were drawn from Ashton Rollins's *The Cowboy*.

world of the range and that of "business," with its almost obligatory suit. Typical "dress" vests were fringed buckskin or brown plush with a black braid edging.

Shirts were wool or cotton, pullover style — that is, buttoning partly down the front — and of subdued colors; red was rarely seen. Chaps were skeleton overalls, originally made of cowhide, very stiff and tight, and sometimes called "shotguns." They had no side openings, as in the later "bat-wing" type, which resembled a double skirt clipped at the sides to give more freedom. Leather chaps might have white buckskin fringes or edging. Later developments were fur chaps rather than leather — of bear, wolf, pony, or sheep pelts or angora wool.

Overcoats were made of canvas; they were knee length, often painted to render them windproof. Riding coats of buffalo hide were seen in the early days, and these were worn with fur caps.

According to the Stetson Company in Philadelphia, about 1870 Mr. Stetson produced a wide-brimmed hat, based on what he knew of Western life; this was named "Boss of the Plains" and shipped to trading posts throughout the West. In the southern plains areas of Texas and the Southwest the Stetson had a brim four inches wide and a crown seven inches high; farther north both brim and crown were somewhat smaller. In the Southwest the level-brimmed, high-crowned hat was worn pinched in, while in the North the top crown was dented in all around. The Stetson immediately became popular because it was comfortable, afforded protection against sun and rain, and could, if need be, double as a water carrier or a pillow. Hatbands were made of leather, silver conchas, or sometimes snakeskin.

Neckerchiefs were customary — not for looks but as protection against dust when driving herds. They were usually the plain red bandannas worn in the South.

Gloves were universally worn to protect the hands against rope burns and other hazards. They were of buckskin with flared gauntlet wrists and might be ornately decorated with a spread eagle, Texas star, or silver conchas. In addition to gloves, black or brown leather cuff guards were common.

Boots were of the finest quality black leather, quite loose, and came to just below the knees. Boot heels were traditionally two inches high. As decoration, a concha might be worn in front at the top, and sometimes the leg was decorated with quilted stitching. In periods of great cold, a boot overshoe or arctic was worn over a "German sock," a knee-high stocking of thick felt. Spurs were invariably worn.

War paint — that is, soot grease — was smeared under the eyes as protection against snow glare in the wintry plains regions.

Joe Woods

after Remington

Albert Potter

Fred Sutton

Trail drivers of the '70s

Baptiste Garnier

Teddy Blue

J. D. Smith, foreman

Charlie Russell and friend

Scandinavian pioneer

George Hedderich

O. J. Wiren, rancher

Teddy Roosevelt   Charlie Russell   Ed Willson   Russell   Chuck Pierson

Top hand

John Bowen

Ranchman

Hunter

Sheriff Frank Canton

Hunter

William Cantrell (Flopping Bill)

Canadian ranger

Commodore Perry Owens

c. 1895

Pearl Hart

Bat Masterson

Rose of Cimarron

Charlie Siringo

Stager

Winter gear

1893

Ranch cook

c 1900

J. D. Powell

Typical punchers taking their ease

Texas punchers

David Lant, rustler

Hunters in North Dakota

Rough Rider scout

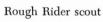

Martin M'Rose and Tom Finnessy

Top hands

Ike Pryor

Pawnee County officer

Agency Indian

Pawnee County officer

235

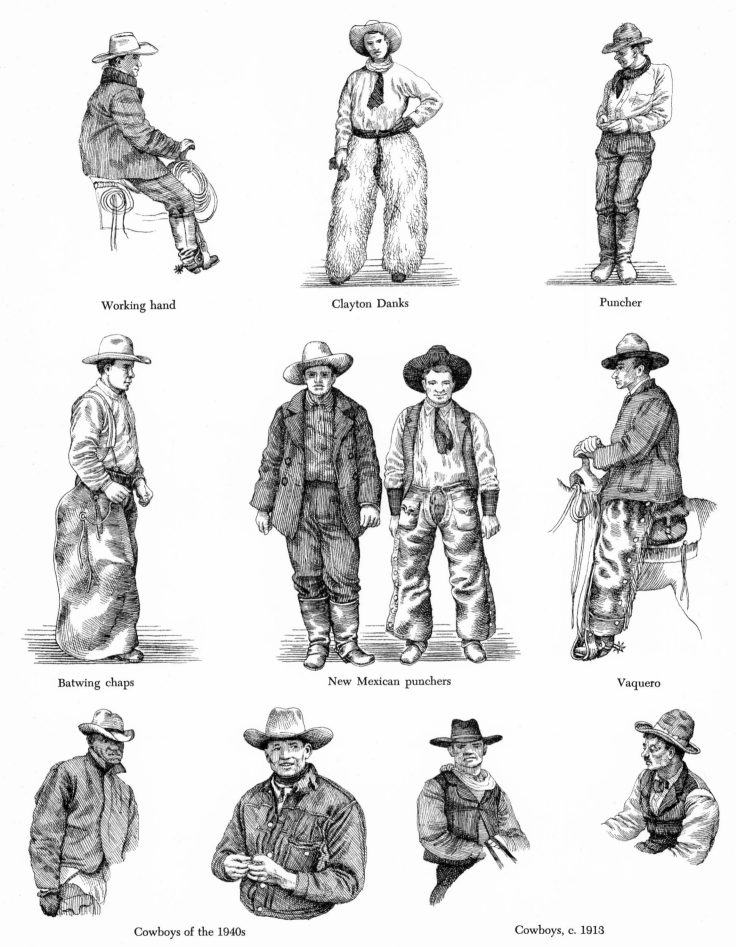

Working hand

Clayton Danks

Puncher

Batwing chaps

New Mexican punchers

Vaquero

Cowboys of the 1940s

Cowboys, c. 1913

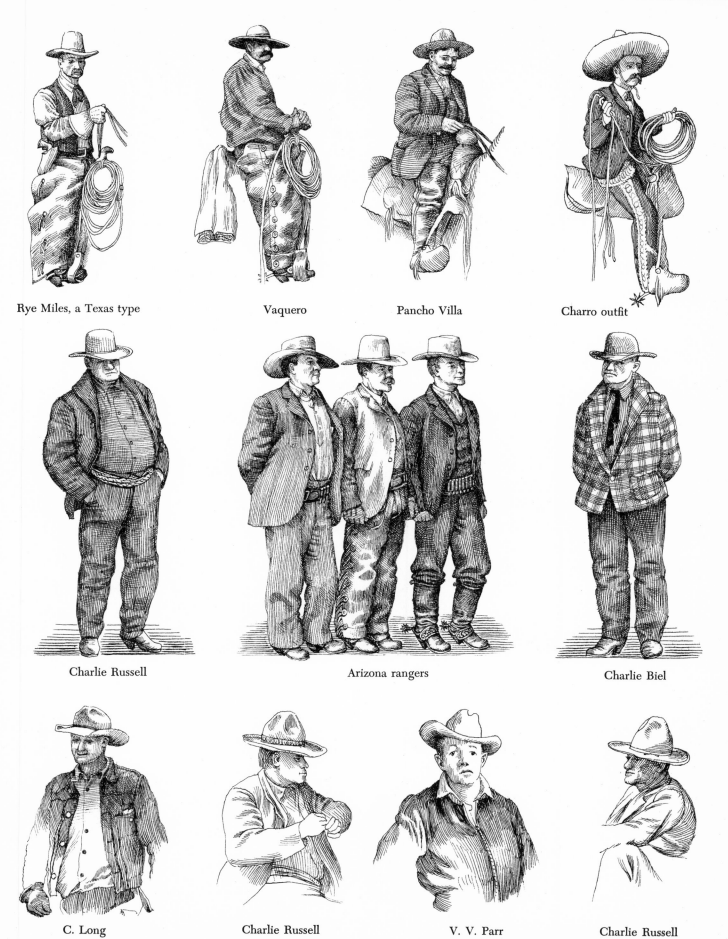

Rye Miles, a Texas type

Vaquero

Pancho Villa

Charro outfit

Charlie Russell

Arizona rangers

Charlie Biel

C. Long

Charlie Russell

V. V. Parr

Charlie Russell

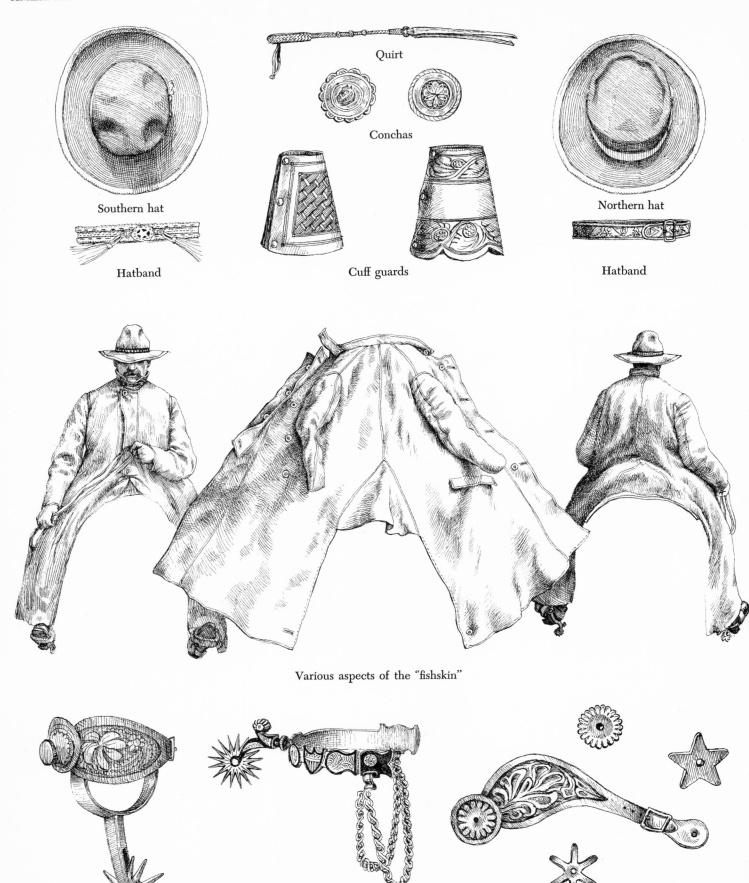

Quirt

Conchas

Southern hat

Northern hat

Hatband

Cuff guards

Hatband

Various aspects of the "fishskin"

Spurs

Spur strap

Rowels

TEDDY ROOSEVELT

The First Quarter of the Twentieth Century

IN AMERICA in the first decade of the twentieth century there was little elegance in clothing. There were a few occasions of great sartorial display, such as was seen at the Marlborough-Vanderbilt wedding, but on the whole this embraced only a very small New York-Newport clique. The real America, that of the great middle class — which by now included almost everyone — acquiesced to the ugly women's styles passed on by the Parisian fashion enterprises.

Men's upstanding, starched collars, starched cuffs, straw hats, and fedoras gave to the prewar years a typical chairman-of-the-board look. The derby remained for some years, and the English raincoat came to stay. Never, perhaps, was upper-class clothing — respectable, affluent, and impractical — more generally worn.

In women's dress, the puffed-sleeve, bosomy look of the '90s gradually changed into the slope-shouldered, shapeless dresses of World War I. Women adopted monkey fur, silver-fox fur pieces, kettle hats, flared coats, and unattractive fur borders.

During the war women's skirts rose rather quickly, in preparation for the exaggerated styles to follow. At the same time belts were lowered well below the normal waistline. Laboring under these handicaps, women nevertheless tried to appear as *femmes fatales*. During the same period men were tightly encased in buttoned coats and narrow, rather short, cuffed trousers. These, in turn, were displaced by the raccoon coats and collegiate clownishness of the Jazz Age.

But great movements were afoot. In 1920, with the ratification of the Nineteenth Amendment, women gained the privilege of equal suffrage. With this prerogative their social and economic horizons were vastly broadened. During the war many of them had worked on equal footing with men, and now that the war years were over they saw no need — and many had no desire — to return to the more "genteel" occupations formerly open to them.

This sudden economic upheaval, one perhaps more revolutionary than is generally realized, was influential in causing a drastic change in clothing fashions. In the years 1925-1930 women did their best to deny their essential femininity: skirts were raised above the knees, breasts were concealed, hips were minimized by lowering the waistline. Even hair was clipped to "boyish bobs" or was shingled in imitation of men. Not since the period of the French Revolution had styles reached such extremes.

Paris, New York, and Hollywood had become the three major style centers. But one common sentiment prevailed throughout the clothing industry: the conviction that CHANGE be introduced as frequently as possible.

Historical Survey

1903: The Wright brothers, Wilbur and Orville, made the first successful flight in a motor-powered airplane at Kitty Hawk, N. C. Ford Motor Company established by Henry Ford (1863-1947).

1903: *The Call of the Wild,* by Jack London (1876-1916).

1903: "Mother and Child" (in Worcester Art Museum), by Mary Cassatt (1845-1926).

1907: "Cavalry Charge on a Southern Plain in 1860," by Frederic Remington (1861-1909), painter, illustrator, and sculptor.

1909: Robert E. Peary (1856-1920) reached the North Pole.

1914: Panama Canal opened.

1914-18: World War I.

1918: Fourteen Points outlined by President Woodrow Wilson (1856-1924).

My Antonia, by Willa Cather (1876-1947).

1920: First Assembly of the League of Nations in Geneva (United States not represented). Prohibition and Women's Suffrage amendments went into effect.

Main Street, by Sinclair Lewis (1885-1951).

1922: *The Waste Land,* by T. S. Eliot (1882- —), poet and critic.

1923: *Rhapsody in Blue,* by George Gershwin (1898-1937).

1925: *The Great Gatsby,* by F. Scott Fitzgerald (1896-1940).

Three ladies

Lillian Russell

Wedding guests

William Collier

after William Paxton

Alice Roosevelt Longworth

Maude Knowlton

1908

1908

1900

Actress

The business suit at its height

Four fashionable ladies

Fashionable dress of the war and postwar periods

Fashions in hats and fur pieces

Evening dress

Women adopt the suit

Marilyn Miller

The disappearing waist

Femme fatale

c. 1919

Some of those hats

Where are the waists of yesteryear?

The new woman in Hollywood

The Fitzgerald era

Bibliography

COSTUME OF THE ANCIENT WORLD *and* EUROPEAN COSTUME
Numbers indicate call numbers in the Metropolitan Museum of Art Library, New York City

Abrahams, Ethel B. *Greek Dress*. London: J. Murray, 1908. 234.14, Ab8

Album des costumes de la cour de Rome. Paris: Silvestre, 1862. 237.7, H361

d'Allemagne, Henry René. *Les Accessoires du costume et du mobilier depuis le treizième jusqu' au milieu du dixneuvième siècle*. Paris: Schemit, 1928. 3 vols. 159, Al5.1

Archäologisches Institut des deutschen Reiches. *Abteilung Athen. Mittelungen*. Berlin: 1876-1940. 565, D49

L'Art et la mode (magazine). 233.4, Ar7.Q

Ashdown, Mrs. Charles H. *British Costume During* xix *Centuries*. London: T. C. & E. C. Jack, 1910. 233.1, As3

Bastard, Auguste, comte de. *Costumes de la cour de Bourgogne sous le règne de Philippe* iii *dit Le Bon*. Paris: Imprimerie Nationale, 1881. 233.4, B29.Q

Baudelaire, Pierre Charles. *The Painter of Victorian Life: A Study of Constantin Guys*. London: The Studio, Ltd., 1930. 187G99, B32

La Belle assemblée (magazine). London: J. Bell, 1816-27. 233.12, B41

Beltrami, Luca. *L'Arte negli arredi sacri della Lombardia*. Milan: U. Hoepli, 1897. 113.21, B41.Q

Bertrand de Moleville, Antoine, marquis de. *Costume of the Hereditary States of the House of Austria*. London: W. Miller, 1804. 233.31, B46.Q

Bieber, Margarete. *Entwicklungsgeschichte der griechischen tracht*. Berlin: Gebr. Mann, 1934. 231.14, B472

Blum, André. *Histoire du costume*. Paris: Hachette, 1928. 233.4, B62

——. *L'Œuvre gravé d'Abraham Bosse*. Paris: A. Morancé, 1924. 2 vols. 201.6, B65, B62

Bock, Franz. *Die Kleinodien des heil. romischen Reiches deutscher Nation*. Vienna: Hof- und Staatsdruckerei, 1864. 233.3, B63.F

——. *Geschichte des liturgischen Gewänder des Mittelalters*. Bonn: Henry & Cohen, 1859-71. 237.7, B63

von Boehn, Max. *Das Beiwerk der Mode*. Munich: F. Bruckman A.-G., 1928. 231, B631

——. *Modes and Manners of the Nineteenth Century*. London: J. M. Dent & Sons; New York: E. P. Dutton and Co., 1927. 4 vols. 231, B635

——. *Rokoko, Frankreich im* xviii. *Jahrhundert*. Berlin: Askanischer Verlag, 1921. 110.4, B631

——. *Vom Kaiserreich zur Republik*. Munich: Hyperionverlag, 1921. 230.32, B63

Bonnard, Camillo. *Costumi dei secoli* xiii, xiv *e* xv. Milan: 1832-35. 2 vols. 231.3, B64

Bouchot, Henri François. *L'Épopée du costume militaire française*. Paris: Société française d'éditions d'art, 1898. 237.5, B66

——. *Le Luxe française — la Restauration*. Paris: a la Librarie illustrée, 1893. 230.32, B66

Braun, Joseph. *Die liturgische Gewandung im Occident und Orient*. Freiburg im Breisgau, and St. Louis, Mo.; B. Herder, 1907. 237.7 B73

Capart, Jean. *L'Art et la parure féminine dans l'ancienne Égypte*. Brussels: Vromant, 1907. 231.12, C17

Carré, Jean Baptiste Louis. *Panoplie*. Paris: Fuchs, 1795. 147.1, C23

Challamel, Jean Baptiste Augustin. *The History of Fashion in France*. London: Low, Marston and Co., 1882. 233.4, C35

Chancellor, E[dwin] Beresford. *Life in Regency and Early Victorian Times*. London: B. T. Batsford, Ltd., 1926.

Les Chapeaux du très parisien (magazine). Paris: 1921-36. 233.4, C361.Q

Clayton, Henry J. *Ornaments of the Ministers as Shown on English Monumental Brasses*. Milwaukee: Morehouse; London: A. R. Mowbray, 1919. 237.7, C57

Clayton, Muriel. *Catalogue of Rubbings of Brasses and Incised Slabs* (in Victoria and Albert Museum). London: Board of Education publication, 1929. 147.3, V662

Clinch, George. *English Costume from Prehistoric Times to the End of the Eighteenth Century*. London: Methuen, 1909; Chicago: A. C. McClurg, 1910. 233.12, C61

Costumes de cour (French). 233.4, C82

Creccelius, Joannes. *Collectanea de Origine et*

Fundatione Omnium ferè Monasticorum Ordinum in Specie. Francofurti: 1614. 947, C86

Cunnington, Cecil Willett. *English Women's Clothing in the Nineteenth Century.* London: Faber & Faber, Ltd., 1937. 233.12, C91

Dandré-Bardon, Michel. *Costume des anciens peuples.* Paris: A. Jombert, 1784-86. 21.1, B231

Davenport, Millia. *The Book of Costume.* New York: Crown Publishers, 1948. 2 vols. 231, D27

Day, T. A., and Dines, J. H. *Illustrations of Mediæval Costume in England.* London: T. Bosworth, 1853. 233.12, D33

Dayot, Armand Pierre Marie. *De la Régence à la Révolution: la vie française au xviiie siècle.* Paris: E. Flammarion, no date. 230.32, D338

——. *La Révolution française.* Paris: E. Flammarion, 1897. 230.32, D33

Dillon, Harold A. L. *Pageant of the Birth, Life, and Death of . . . Earl of Warwick K. G. 1389-1439.* New York and London: Longmans Green and Co., 1914. 272.3, D58

Disher, M[aurice] Willson. *Music Hall Parade.* London: B. T. Batsford, Ltd.; New York: Charles Scribner's Sons, 1938.

Doyé, Franz von Sales. *Die alten Trachten der männlichen und weiblichen Orden.* Leipzig: Vier Quellen Verlag, 1930. 237.7, D77

Druitt, Herbert. *A Manual of Costume as Illustrated by Monumental Brasses.* London: A. Moring, Ltd., 1906. 147.3, D84

Duplessis, Georges. *Costumes historiques des xvie, xviie et xviiie siècles.* Paris: A. Lévy, 1867. 2 vols. 21.4, D92

Earle, Alice Morse. *Two Centuries of Costume in America,* London and New York: The Macmillan Co., 1903. 2 vols. 236.5, Ea7

Enlart, Camille. *Manuel d'archéologie française.* Paris: A. Picard, 1902-16. 3 vols. 110.4, En5

von Falke, Jakob. *Costümgeschichte der Culturvölker.* Stuttgart: W. Spemann, 1880. 231, F18

Ferrari, Filippo. *Costumi ecclesiastici, civili e militari della corte di Roma.* Rome: L. Nicoletti, 1823. 233.5, F41

Ferrario, Giulio. *Il Costume antico e moderno.* Florence: V. Batelli, 1823-37. 35 vols. 231, F41

Fischel, Oskar. *Chronisten der Mode, Mensch und Kleid in Bildern.* Potsdam: Müller and Co., 1923. 231, F52

Floerke, Hanns. *Die Moden der italienischen Renaissance.* Munich: Georg Müller, 1917. 233.5, F652

Forestier, Amédée. *The Roman Soldier.* London:

A. & C. Black, Ltd.; New York: The Macmillan Co., 1928. 237.5, F76

French Fashions for Women of 1867-72; a scrapbook. 233.4, F884.Q

——. c. 1890. 233.4, F882.

Friedländer, Max J. *Die Gemalde von Lucas Cranach.* Berlin: Deutscher Verein für Kunstwissenschaft, 1932. 179C85, F91

Galerie des modes et costumes français, dessinés d'après nature, 1778-87. Paris: É. Lévy, 1911-12. 4 vols. 233.4, G13.Q

La Gazette de la Reine pour l'année 1782. Paris: 1925. 233.4, G251.Q

Gazette du bon ton. Paris: 1912-25. 233.4, G25

Genoni, Rosa. *La Storia della moda attraverso i secoli.* Bergamo: Instituto italiano d'arti grafiche, c. 1925. 231, G28

Geszler, J. *Les Modes du xixe siècle.* Paris: P. Ollendorff, 189?. 233, G33

Goetz, Walter. *Das Mittelalter bis zum Ausgang der Staufer, 400-1250.* Berlin: Im Propylden-Verlag, 1932. 900.1, P94, v 3

——. *Das Zeitalter der Gotik und Renaissance 1250-1500.* Berlin: Im Propylden-Verlag, 1932. 900.1, P94, v 4

Goldscheider, Ludwig. *Roman Portraits.* New York: Oxford University Press, 1940. 617, G57.Q

Gosse, A. Bothwell. *The Civilization of the Ancient Egyptians.* London: T. C. & E. C. Jack, 1915; New York: F. Stokes and Co., 1916. 535, G69

Grand-Carteret, John. *L'Histoire, la vie, les mœurs, et la curiosité . . . 1450-1900.* Paris: Librarie de la curiosité et des beaux-arts, 1927-28. 5 vols. 230, G76

Graphical Representation of the Coronation Regalia of the Kings of England. 233.12, G76

Grose, Francis. *Military Antiquities Respecting . . . the English Army from the Conquest to the Present Time.* London: S. Hooper, 1786-88. 2 vols. 237.5, G91

Guillaumot, Auguste E. *Costumes of the Time of the French Revolution. 1790-1793.* New York: J. W. Bouton, 1889. 231.4 G94.Q

Hamilton, Sir William. *Recueil de gravures d'après des vases antiques.* Paris: Bénard, 1803-1809. 4 vols. 579.2, H185, F

Hampe, Theodor E. *Das Trachtenbuch des Christoph Weiditz.* Berlin and Leipzig: W. de Gruyter and Co., 1927. 233.3, H18

Harmand, Adrien. *Jeanne d'Arc, ses costumes, son armure.* Paris: E. Leroux, 1929. 233.4, H22

Hartley, Dorothy. *Mediæval Costume and Life.* London: B. T. Batsford, Ltd., 1931; New York: Charles Scribner's Sons, 1932. 233.12, H25

Hartley, Dorothy, and Elliot, Margaret M. *Life and Work of the People of England*. New York and London: G. P. Putnam's Sons, 1926-31. 6 vols. 230.23, H25

von Hefner-Alteneck, Jakob H. *Costumes du moyen-âge chrétien d'apres des monuments contemporains*. Frankfort: H. Keller, 1840-54. 3 vols. 231.2, H36

Hélyot, Pierre. *Histoire des ordres monastiques, religieux et militaires*. Paris: N. Gosselin, 1714-19. 947, H36

Heuzey, Léon A. *Histoire du costume dans l'antiquité classique*. Paris: Les Belles Lettres, 1935. 231.1, H484

Hinz, A. *Die Schatzkammer der Marienkirche zu Danzig*. Danzig: A. W. Kafeman, 1870. 156.35, H59

Honourable Artillery Company, 1537-1937. London, W & S, Ltd., 1937. 955.5, H75

Hope, Thomas. *Costume of the Ancients*. London: H. G. Bohn, 1841. 2 vols. 231.1, H77

Hottenroth, Friedrich. *Handbuch der deutschen Tracht*. Stuttgart: G. Weise, 1892-96. 233.3, H792

Houston, Mary G. *Medieval Costume in England and France, the 13th, 14th, and 15th Centuries*. London: A. & C. Black Ltd., 1939; New York: The Macmillan Co., 1940. 231, H81, v 3

Houston, Mary G., and Hornblower, F. S. *Ancient Egyptian, Assyrian, and Persian Costumes and Decorations*. London: A. & C. Black, Ltd., 1920; New York: The Macmillan Co., 1921. 231, H81, v 1

——. *Ancient Greek, Roman, and Byzantine Costume and Decoration*. London: A. & C. Black, Ltd.; New York: The Macmillan Co., 1931. 231, H81, v 2

Hughes, Talbot. *Dress Design*. New York: The Macmillan Co., 1913; London: Sir I. Pitman & Sons, 1920. 233.12, H87

The Illustrated London News. Dec. 4, 1937. 018, 1L6.Q

Jefferys, Thomas. *A Collection of the Dresses of Different Nations, Ancient and Modern, Particularly Old English Dresses*. London: T. Jefferys, 1757-72. 4 vols. 231, J36

Kelly, Francis M., and Schwabe, Randolph. *Historic Costume*. London: B. T. Batsford, Ltd., 1925; New York: Charles Scribner's Sons, 1930. 233, K29

——. *A Short History of Costume and Armour*. London: B. T. Batsford, Ltd.; New York: Charles Scribner's Sons, 1931. 233, K292

Klassiker der Kunst in Gesamtausgaben. Stuttgart and Leipzig: Deutsche Verlags-Anstalt, 1904- ——. 38 vols.

Köhler, Karl. *A History of Costume*. Philadelphia: David McKay Co., 1937. 231, K822.

Kromayer, Johannes, and Veith, Georg. *Heerwesen und Kriegführung der Griechen und Romer*. Munich: C. H. Beck, 1928. 560, M91, v 4, pt 32

Lacroix, Paul. *Mœurs, usages, et costumes au moyen âge et à l'époque de la Renaissance*. Paris: Firmin-Didot, 1877. 231.2, L114

The Lady's Friend (Mrs. Henry Peterson, ed.). Philadelphia: 1886. vol. 3. 236.5, L123

Lagrelius, Axel. *Kongl. Livrustkammaren och dermed forenade samlinger*. Stockholm: 1897-1901. 147.1, St6, 624.Q

Lawson, Cecil C. *A History of the Uniforms of the British Army*. London: P. Davies, 1940-41. 237.5, L44

Lecomte, Hippolyte. *Costumes civiles et militaires de la monarchie française depuis 1200 jusqu'à 1820*. Paris: F. Delpech, 1820. 233.4, L49.

Lécuyer, Raymond. *Histoire de la photographie*. Paris: Baschet et cie., 1945.

von Leitner, Quirin (ed.). *Freydal; des Kaisers Maximilian 1, Turniere und Mummereien*. Vienna: A. Holzhausen, 1880-82. 2 vols. 147.1, L53.Q

Leloir, Maurice. *Histoire du costume de l'antiquité à 1914*. Paris: Henri Ernst, 1933-38. 11 vols. 231, L53

Limbourg, Pol de. *Les Très riches heures du duc de Berry* (text by Henri Malo). Paris: Éditions de la revue Verve, 1940. 100.52, V612.Q,no.7-8

La Lingerie du "Très parisien." Paris: 1926-32. 233.4, L64

Linthicum, M(arie) Channing. *Costume in the Drama of Shakespeare and His Contemporaries*. Oxford: Clarendon Press, 1936. 233.1, L65

Luard, John. *A History of the Dress of the British Soldier, from the Earliest Period to the Present Time*. London: W. Clowes, 1852. 237.5, L96

Lutz, Henry F. *Textiles and Costumes among the Peoples of the Ancient Near East*. Leipzig: J. C. Hinrichs; New York: G. E. Stechert and Co., 1923. 156.4, L97

MacDonald, R. J. *History of the Dress of the Royal Regiment of Artillery, 1625-1897*. London: H. Sotheran, 1899. 237.5, M14

Malliot, Joseph. *Recherches sur les costumes . . . des anciens peuples*. Paris: P. Martin, 1909. 3 vols. 231.1, M29

Mannowsky, Walter. *Der Danziger Paramentenschatz . . . aus der Marienkirche*. Berlin: Brandussche Verlagsbuchhandlung, 1931-33. 3 vols. 156.35, M31.Q

Meyers, Charles L. *Bibliography of Colonial Costume Compiled for the Society of Colonial Wars in the State of New Jersey.* New York: 1923. 236.5, M57

Meyrick, Sir Samuel R. *A Critical Inquiry into Ancient Armour . . . from the Norman Conquest to the Reign of King Charles II.* London: R. Jennings, 1824. 3 vols. 147.1, M57.Q

Meyrick, Sir Samuel R., and Smith, Charles H. *The Costume of the Original Inhabitants of the British Isles from the Earliest Periods to the Sixth Century.* London: R. Havell, 1815. 231.1, M57.Q

La Mode chic (magazine). 1936-39. 233.4, M724

La Mode pratique (magazine). Vols. 9-11, 1900-1902. 233.4, M726.Q

Les Modes (magazine). Vols. 7-20, 1907-23. 233.4, M722

Modes de Paris du petit courrier des dames. Paris: 1863-64. 233.4, M72

de Montfaucon, Bernard. *L'Antiquité expliquée et représentée en figures.* Paris: F. Delaulne, 1722 (2d ed.). 5 vols. 500, M76.Q

Morazzoni, Giuseppe. *La Moda a Venezia nel secolo XVIII.* Milan: Amici del museo teatrale alla Scala, 1931. 233.5, M79

Morse, Harriet K. *Elizabethan Pageantry.* London and New York: The Studio, 1934. 233.12, M83

Nelson, Henry L. *Army of the United States.* Vol. 2: *Uniform of the, 1898-1907.* Facsimile plates from water-color drawings by Henry A. Ogden. New York: no date. 2 vols. 237.5, N33.Q

Norris, Herbert. *Costume and Fashion.* London: J. M. Dent & Sons, Ltd.; New York: E. P. Dutton and Co., 1924-39. 4 vols. 231, N79

Paris Exposition universelle, 1900. Musée rétrospectif des classes 85 & 86. *Le costume et ses accessoires.* St. Cloud: 1900. 233.4, P214

Paris Musée des Arts décoratifs; Les Nouvelles collections. *Le Costume.* Vol. 17, 233.4, P21

Pauquet, Polydore. *Modes et costumes historiques.* Paris: Pauquet frères, 1862. 233.4, P28.

Philippi, Friedrich. *Atlas zur weltlichen Altertumskunde des deutschen Mittelalters.* Bonn and Leipzig: K. Schroeder, 1924. 11.3, P53.Q

Picart, Bernard. *Cérémonies et coutumes réligieuses de tous les peuples du monde.* Amsterdam: J. F. Bernard, 1723-43. 11 vols. 940.1, P58.Q

Piton, Camille. *Le Costume civil en France du XIIIe au XIXe siècle.* Paris: E. Flammarion, 1913. 233.4 P68

Planché, James R. *Costumes of Shakespeare's Historical Play of King Henry the Fourth.* London: J. Miller, 1824. 237.8, P69

Polidori Calamandrei, E. *Le vesti delle donne fiorentine nel quattrocento.* Florence: "La Voce," 1924. 233.5, C12

Price, Julius M. *Dame Fashion, Paris-London (1786-1912).* London: Low, Marston, and Co., Ltd.; New York: Charles Scribner's Sons, 1913. 237.1, P93

Pronti, Domenico. *Nuova raccolta rappresentante i costumi religiosi, civili, e militari degli antichi Egiziani, Etruschi, Greci, e Romani. . . .* Rome: 1800? 231.1, P94

Pugin, Augustus W. *Glossary of Ecclesiastical Ornament and Costume.* London: B. Quaritch, 1868. 153.8, P962

Pyne, William H. *The Costume of Great Britain.* London: W. Miller, 1808. 233.1, P992.Q

——. *England, Scotland, and Ireland, a Description of the . . . Customs, Dress. . . .* London: 1827. 4 vols. 233.1, P99

Quicherat, Jules. *Histoire du costume en France . . . jusqu'à la fin du XVIIIe siècle.* Paris: Hachette, 1877. 233.4, Qu4

Racinet, Albert C. A. *Le Costume historique.* Paris: Firmin-Didot et cie, 1876-88. 6 vols. 231, R11—Ref.

Reiset, Gustave. *Modes et usages au temps de Marie-Antoinette.* Paris: Firmin-Didot et cie., 1885. 2 vols. 233.4, R27

Repond, Jules. *Le Costume de la Garde suisse pontificale et la Renaissance italienne.* Rome: Polyglotte Vaticane, 1917. 233.5, R29

Roger-Milès, Léon. *Comment discerner les styles du VIIIe au XIXe siècle.* Vol. 3: *Le costume et la mode.* Paris: G. Baranger fils, 1896-99. 110.4, R63.3

Roulin, Eugène A. *Vestments and Vesture.* London: Sands & Co.; St. Louis, Mo.: B. Herder, 1931. 237.7, R75

Rudnitzki, Paul. *Der Turnierroman "Livre des faits du bon chevalier Messire Jacques de Lalaing."* Münster in Westf.: Aschendorff, 1915. 272.1, R83

Ruppert, Jacques. *Le Costume.* Paris: R. Ducher, 1930-31. 231, R87

Schoonebeek, Adriaan. *Histoire des ordres réligieux de l'un et de l'autre sexe.* Amsterdam: H. Desbordes, 1695-1700. 2 vols. 237.7, Sch6

Schrenk, Jacobus. *Der aller durchleuchtigisten und grosmachtigen Kayser.* Ynszprugg: 1603. 147.1 Aml, C244, F

Schwan, Christian F. *Abbildungen der vorzüglich-*

sten geistlichen-Orden in ihren gewohnlichsten Ordenskleidungen. Mannheim: C. F. Schwan & C. B. Gotz, 1791. 2 vols. 237.7, Sch9

Shaw, Henry. *Dresses and Decorations of the Middle Ages.* London: W. Pickering, 1843. 2 vols. 231.2, Sh2

Sitwell, Sacheverell. *Conversation Pieces.* London: B. T. Batsford, Ltd.; New York: Charles Scribner's Sons, 1937. 188, Si8

——. *Narrative Pictures.* London: B. T. Batsford, Ltd.; New York: Charles Scribner's Sons, 1938. 188, Si82

Society for Army Historical Research. *Journal.* Sheffield, England: 1921-46. 24 vols. 147.18, So1

Stirling-Maxwell, Sir William. *The Procession of Pope Clement* VII *and the Emperor Charles* V *after the Coronation . . . February* MDXXX. Designed and engraved by Nicolas Hogenberg and reproduced in facsimile. Edinburgh: Edmonston & Douglas, 1875. 185H67, Y, F

Stothard, Charles A. *The Monumental Effigies of Great Britain from the Norman Conquest to the Reign of Henry* VIII. London: 1817. 138.4, St7.Q

Strutt, Joseph. *A Complete View of the Dress and Habits of the People of England.* London: H. G. Bohn, 1842. 2 vols. 233.12, St82

——. *The Regal and Ecclesiastical Antiquities of England . . . from Edward the Confessor to Henry the Eighth.* London: H. G. Bohn, 1842. 233.12, St84

Thibault, Girard. *Académie de l'espée.* Antwerp: 1628. 240.7, T344, F

van Thienen, Frithjof. *Das Kostüm der Blütezeit Hollands, 1600-1660.* Berlin: Deutscher Kunstverlag, 1930. 233.92, T34

Truman, Nevil. *Historic Costuming.* London: Sir I. Pitman, 1936. 231, T77

Tuer, Andrew W. *The Follies and Fashions of Our Grandfathers (1807).* London: Field & Tuer, 1886-87. 233.1, T81

Uzanne, (Louis) Octave. *Fashion in Paris . . . 1797 to 1897.* London: W. Heinemann; New York: Charles Scribner's Sons, 1898. 233.4, Uz1

Vecellio, Cesare. *Costumes anciens et modernes.* Paris: Firmin-Didot frères, 1860. 2 vols. 231, V49

van Velsen, Gerard. *Waare afbeeldingen van de hollandse graaven en gravinnen.* Haarlem?: c. 1600. 201.5, V54.Q

Vever, Henri. *La Bijouterie française au* XIXe *siècle.* Paris: H. Floury, 1906-08. 3 vols. 146, V64

Viel-Castel, Horace, comte de. *Collection des costumes, armes et meubles.* Paris: Treuttel & Wurtz, 1827-45. 4 vols. 233.4, V67.Q

de Vigne, Félix. *Recherches historiques sur les costumes civils et militaires des gildes et des corporations et métiers. . . .* Gand: F. & E. Gyselynck, 1847. 953, V68

——. *Vade-mecum de peintre, ou, Recueil de costumes du moyen-âge.* Brussels: L. Jorez, 1835. 233.93, V68.Q

van Vinkeroy, E. *Costumes militaires belges du* XIe *au* XVIII *siècle.* Braine-le-Comte: Lelong, 1885. 147.1 V37

Violett-le-Duc, Eugène E. *Dictionnaire raisonné du mobilier français de l'époque carlovingienne à la renaissance.* Paris: Bance, 1858-75. 6 vols. 159.16, V81

Waller, John G. and L. A. B. *A Series of Monumental Brasses from the Thirteenth to the Sixteenth Century.* London: J. B. Nichols, 1864. 147.3, W15.Q

Wendel, Friedrich. *Weib und Mode, eine Sittengeschichte im Spiegel der Karikatur.* Dresden: P. Aretz Verlag, 1928. 273, W48

Williams, Franklin B., Jr. *Elizabethan England.* Boston: Museum of Fine Arts, c. 1939. 108.1, B65, M992, Q no. 1

Witte, Fritz. *Die liturgischen Gewander und kirchlichen Stickereien des Schnütgenmuseums Koln.* Berlin: Verlag für Kunstwissenschaft, 1926. 156.35, W78.Q

Bibliography

AMERICAN COSTUME

Numbers indicate call numbers in the New York Public Library reference room.

Abbott, Edward C. *We Pointed Them North.* New York: Farrar and Rinehart, Inc., 1939. AN (Abbott, E.)

Abbott, Henry. *North Bay Brook.* New York: published by the author, 1929. MYER

Adams, R. F., and Britzman, H. E. *Charles M. Russell, the Cowboy Artist.* Pasadena, Cal.: Trail's End Publishing Co., 1948. MCX R/+ 96.A3

Aikman, Duncan. *Calamity Jane and the Lady Wildcats.* New York: Henry Holt and Co., 1937. IW

Ayers, Nathaniel M. *Building a New Empire.* New York, Chicago: Broadway Publishing Co., 1910. IW

Babb, Theodore A. *In the Bosom of the Comanches.* Amarillo, Texas: T. A. Babb, 1923. HBC

Beebe, Lucius M., and Clegg, Charles. *U. S. West, the Saga of Wells Fargo.* New York: E. P. Dutton and Co., 1949. TNK (Wells)

Bell, Katherine M. *Swinging the Censer.* Santa Barbara, Cal.: 1931. AN (Bell, K.)

Birney, Hoffman. *Vigilantes.* Philadelphia: The Penn Publishing Co., 1929. IWL

Blake, Forrester. *Riding the Mustang Trail.* New York: Charles Scribner's Sons, 1935. IWR

Blanchard, Leola H. *Conquest of Southwest Kansas.* Wichita, Kan.: Wichita Eagle Press, 1931. IWA

Bratt, John. *Trails of Yesterday.* Chicago: University Publishing Co., 1921. AN

Brown, Jesse, and Willard, A. M. *The Black Hills Trails.* Rapid City, S. Dak.: Rapid City Journal Co., 1924. IWE

Bryson, Nettie K. *Prairie Days.* Los Angeles: Times-Mirror, 1939. AN (Bryson, N.)

Burdick, Usher L. *Tales from Buffalo Land.* Baltimore: Wirth Brothers, 1940. IWG

Burgum, Jessamine. *Zezula, or Pioneer Days in the Smoky Water Country.* Valley City, N. Dak.: Gretchell & Nielsen, 1937. IWE

Burnham, Frederick R. *Taking Chances.* Los Angeles: Haynes Corp., 1944. AN (Burnham, F.)

Butcher, S. D. *Pioneer History of Custer County.* Broken Bow, Neb.: S. D. Butcher & E. S. Finch, 1901. IWD

Butterfield, Roger P. *The American Past.* New York: Simon & Schuster, 1947. IAG/+

California Historical Society Papers. San Francisco: 1887-93. 10 vols. IAA

Callison, John J. *Bill Jones of Paradise Valley, Oklahoma.* Chicago: M. A. Donohue and Co., 1914. AN (Callison, J.)

Canton, Frank M. (E. E. Dale, ed.). *Frontier Trails.* Boston and New York: Houghton Mifflin Co., 1930. AN (Canton, F.)

Carter, Kate B. *Heart Throbs of the West.* Salt Lake City, Utah: Daughters of Utah Pioneers, 1939-48. 9 vols. IXC

Cherry, Edgar, and Company. *Redwood and Lumbering in California Forests.* San Francisco: E. Cherry & Co., 1884. VQY

Chronicles of Oklahoma. Oklahoma City, Okla.: 1921-date. IAA (Oklahoma)

Collins, Libby. *The Cattle Queen of Montana.* Spokane, Wash.: Dyer Printing Co., 1912. *KF (1912)

Commercial Club of Chicago. *A History of the Pilgrimage of the Chicago Commercial Club to Centres of Western Commerce.* Chicago: R. R. Donnelley & Sons Co., 1901. IW

Cook, James H. *Fifty Years on the Old Frontier.* New Haven, Conn.: Yale University Press, 1923. AN (Cook, J.)

Coolidge, Dane. *Fighting Men of the West.* New York: E. P. Dutton and Co., Inc., 1932. AGZ

——. *Old California Cowboys.* New York: E. P. Dutton and Co., Inc., 1939. IW

——. *Texas Cowboys.* New York: E. P. Dutton and Co., Inc., 1937. ITR

Cox, James. *My Native Land.* Philadelphia: Blair Publishing Co., 1903. ILD

Crawford, Lewis F. *Rekindling Camp Fires.* Bismarck, N. Dak.: Capital Book Co., 1926. AN (Connor)

Cunningham, Eugene. *Triggernometry.* New York: Press of the Pioneers, Inc., 1934. SLG

Dale, Edward E. *Cow Country.* Norman, Okla.: University of Oklahoma Press, 1942. IW

——. *The Range Cattle Industry.* Norman, Okla.: University of Oklahoma Press, 1930. TAK

Dellenbaugh, Frederick S. *Breaking the Wilderness.* New York: G. P. Putnam's Sons, 1905. IW

De Voto, Bernard A. *Across the Wide Missouri.* Boston: Houghton Mifflin Co., 1947. IW

De Wolff, J. H. *Pawnee Bill.* Pawnee Bill's Historic Wild West Co., 1902. AN (Lillie)

Dick, Everett N. *The Sod-House Frontier, 1854-1890.* New York and London: D. Appleton-Century Co., Inc., 1937. IW

Douglas, Claude L. *Cattle Kings of Texas.* Dallas, Texas: C. Baugh, 1939. ITR

——. *The Gentlemen in the White Hats.* Dallas, Texas: South-West Press, 1934. ITR

Drury, Clifford M. *Elkana and Mary Walker.* Caldwell, Idaho: The Caxton Printers, Ltd., 1940. HBM (Walker)

Dunn, John B. *Perilous Trails of Texas.* Dallas, Texas: Southwest Press, 1932. AN (Dunn, J.)

Early Western Photographs, 1857-99. Photostat reproductions of 35 photographs in the possession of the *Express Messenger, N. Y. C.* IWC/+

Early Western Prints and Photographs (photostats). IW/+

Epperson, Harry A. *Colorado as I Saw It.* Kaysville, Utah: Inland Printing Co., 1944. IWP

Erskine, Gladys S. *Broncho Charlie.* New York: Thomas Y. Crowell Co., 1934. AN (Miller, C.)

Gard, Wayne. *Frontier Justice.* Norman, Okla.: University of Oklahoma Press, 1949. IW

Goodrich, Frances L. *Mountain Homespun.* New Haven, Conn.: Yale University Press; London: Oxford University Press, 1931. MNE

Goodrich, Lloyd. *Thomas Eakins, His Life and Work.* New York: Whitney Museum of American Art, 1933. MCX E12. G6

Guernsey, Charles A. *Wyoming Cowboy Days.* New York: G. P. Putnam's Sons, 1936. AN (Guernsey, C.)

Gunn, Lewis C. *Records of a California Family.* San Diego, Cal.: 1928. IXG

Guyer, James S. *Pioneer Life in West Texas.* Brownwood, Texas: Published by the author, 1938. ITR

Haley, James Evetts. *Jeff Milton.* Norman, Okla.: University of Oklahoma Press, 1948. AN (Milton, J.)

——. *The XIT Ranch of Texas.* Chicago: Lakeside Press, 1929. °KP (Lakeside)

Hamner, Laura V. *Short Grass and Longhorns.* Norman, Okla.: University of Oklahoma Press, 1943. VPO

Hayne, M. H. E. *The Pioneers of the Klondyke.* London: Low, Marston and Co., 1897. HYG

Higinbotham, John D. *When the West Was Young.* Toronto, Canada: The Ryerson Press, 1933. HY

Hinkle, James F. *Early Days of a Cowboy on the Pecos.* Roswell, N. Mex.: 1937. A p. v. 609

Holbrook, Stewart H. *Holy Old Mackinaw.* New York: The Macmillan Co., 1938. TDK

——. *The Yankee Exodus.* New York: The Macmillan Co., 1950. IQ

Horan, James D. *Desperate Men.* New York: G. P. Putnam's Sons, 1949. SLG

Hough, Emerson. *The Story of the Cowboy.* New York: D. Appleton and Co., 1897. IW

Hudson's Bay Company Series. Toronto, Canada: The Champlain Society, 1938-48. 11 vols. HY

Hunter, John M. *The Trail Drivers of Texas.* Nashville, Tenn.: Cokesbury Press, 1925. ITR

Hynes, William F. *Soldiers of the Frontier.* Denver, Colo.: 1943. HBC

Israelsen, Andrew M. *Utah Pioneering.* Salt Lake City, Utah: Deseret News Press, 1938. AN (Israelsen, A.)

Jackson, Clarence S. *Picture Maker of the Old West, William H. Jackson.* New York: Charles Scribner's Sons, 1947. IW/+

Jackson, Joseph H. *Gold Rush Album.* New York: Charles Scribner's Sons, 1949. IXG

Jocknick, Sidney. *Early Days on the Western Slope of Colorado.* Denver, Colo.: Carson-Harper Co., 1913. IWP

Jones, Thomas L. *From the Gold Mine to the Pulpit.* Cincinnati, Ohio: published by the author, 1904. AN

Kronberg, S. J. *Banbrytaren.* Rock Island, Ill.: Pa Forfattarens Forlag, 1906. IV.

Laut, Agnes C. *The Conquest of the Great Northwest.* London: Hodder & Stoughton, 1909. HY

Lockhart, John Washington. *Sixty Years on the Brazos* (compiled by Jonnie L. Wallis). Los Angeles: 1930. AN (Lockhart, J.)

Lorant, Stefan. *Lincoln, His Life in Photographs.* New York: Duell, Sloan & Pearce, 1941. AN/+ (Lincoln, A.)

Lydick, Lotus N. *Varied Experiences of John Lydick and His Family.* Winfield, Kan.: Courier Publishing Co., 1928. A p. v. 322

Maverick, Mary A. *Memoirs.* San Antonio, Texas: Alamo Printing Co., 1921. AN

McCracken, Harold. *Frederic Remington, Artist of the Old West.* Philadelphia: J. P. Lippincott Co., 1947. MCX/+ R 38. M2

McElrath, Thomson P. *A Press Club Outing.* New York: International League of Press Clubs, 1893. NARA/+

Meredith, Roy. *Mr. Lincoln's Camera Man,*

Mathew B. Brady. New York: Charles Scribner's Sons, 1946. AN (Brady, M.)

Morris, Lloyd R. *Not So Long Ago.* New York: Random House, 1949. ILH

Nebraska History Magazine (formerly, *Nebraska History and Record of Pioneer Days*). Lincoln, Nebr.: 1918-date. IAA

O'Brien, Frank G. *Minnesota Pioneer Sketches.* Minneapolis, Minn.: H. H. S. Rowell, 1904. IVL

Panhandle-Plains Historical Review. Canyon, Texas: 1928-date. IAA (Texas)

Patten, William (ed.). *The Book of Sport.* New York: J. F. Taylor and Co., 1901. MVF/+

Philadelphia Photographer (later, *Photographic Journal of America*). Philadelphia: 1864-88.

Pony Express Courier (magazine), Placerville, Cal.: 1935-date. IAA† (California)

Ralph, Julian. *On Canada's Frontier.* London: J. R. Osgood, 1892. HY

Rister, Carl C. *Border Captives.* Norman, Okla.: University of Oklahoma Press, 1940. HBC

Rogers, Agnes. *The American Procession.* New York and London: Harper & Bros., 1933. IAG/+

——. *Women Are Here To Stay.* New York: Harper & Bros., 1949. SNB/+

Rollins, Philip A. *The Cowboy.* New York: Charles Scribner's Sons, 1936. IW

Rollinson, John K. *Wyoming Seattle Trails.* Caldwell, Idaho: The Caxton Printers, Ltd., 1948. IW

Root, Frank A., and Connelley, W. E. *The Overland Stage to California.* Topeka, Kan.: Crane and Co., 1901. IW

Rose, N. H. *Prints from the Rose Collection of Early Western Photographs.* San Antonio, Texas: 1928. IW/+

Rucker, Maude A. *The Oregon Trail and Some of Its Blazers.* New York: W. Neale, 1930. IXI

Sabin, Edwin L. *Kit Carson Days.* Chicago: A. C. McClurg and Co., 1914. HBM (Carson, C.)

The Santa Fe Trail (*Look* magazine, editors). New York: Random House, 1946. IW

Schatz, August H. *Opening a Cow Country.* Ann Arbor, Mich.: Edwards Brothers, Inc. 1939. IWE

Schmitt, Martin F., and Brown, Dee. *Fighting Indians of the West.* New York: Charles Scribner's Sons, 1948. HBC/+

Scott, Harvey W. *History of the Oregon Country.* Cambridge, Mass.: Riverside Press, 1924. 6 vols. IX

Siringo, Charles A. *A Lone Star Cowboy.* Santa Fe, N. Mex.: 1919. AN

——. *Riata and Spurs.* Boston and New York: Houghton Mifflin Co., 1927. AN (Siringo, C.)

Southern Pacific Company. Historical Collection of Photographs, 1863-88 (photostats). El Paso, Texas: 1888(?). IW/+

Stanley, Clark. *The Life and Adventures of the American Cow-Boy.* Providence, R. I.: published by the author, 1897. IAG p. v. 174, no. 8

Sullivan, Mark. *Our Times.* New York: Charles Scribner's Sons, 1927-35. 6 vols. *R-IL

Sutton, Fred E. *Hands Up!* Indianapolis, Ind.: Bobbs-Merrill Co., 1927. IW

Taft, Robert. *Photography and the American Scene.* New York: The Macmillan Co., 1938. *RR-MFC

Taylor, Joseph H. *Kaleidoscopic Lives.* Washburn, N. Dak.: published by the author, 1902. HBC

——. *Sketches of Frontier and Indian Life on the Upper Missouri and Great Plains.* Washburn, N. Dak.: published by the author, 1895. HBC

Thorp, Nathan H., and Clark, N. M. *Pardner of the Wind.* Caldwell, Idaho: The Caxton Printers, Ltd., 1945. AN (Thorp, N.)

Union Pacific Historical Museum. *Early Western Photographs, 1862-1897.* Omaha, Neb.: Union Pacific Historical Museum, 1930. TPS

United States Army War College, Historical Section. *American Indian War Photographs.* Washington, D. C., 1925. HBC/+

Vestal, Stanley. *The Old Santa Fe Trail.* Boston: Houghton Mifflin Co., 1939. IW

Victor, Frances F. *The River of the West.* Hartford, Conn.: Columbian Book Co., 1871. IW

Visscher, William L. *A Thrilling and Truthful History of the Pony Express.* Chicago: Rand, McNally and Co., 1908. IW

Walsh, C. C. *Early Days on the Western Range.* Boston: Sherman, French and Co., 1917. NBI

Webb, Walter P. *The Great Plains.* Boston: Ginn and Co., 1931. IW

Webster, Kimball. *The Gold Seekers of '49.* Manchester, N. H.: Standard Book Co., 1917. IXG

Wistar, Isaac J. *Autobiography.* Philadelphia: The Wistar Institute, 1914. *KF (1914)

Woodbury, John T. *Vermilion Cliffs.* Denver, Colo.: published by the Woodbury Children, 1933. AN (Woodbury, J.)

Woodward, Mary Dodge. *The Checkered Years.* Caldwell, Idaho: The Caxton Printers, Ltd., 1937. AN (Woodward, M.)

Wright, Robert M. *Dodge City, the Cowboy Capital.* Wichita, Kan.: Wichita Eagle Press, 1913. IWB (Dodge City)

Sources for *"Costume of the Ancient World"* and *"European Costume"*

KEY

C. Inst. Costume Institute of the Metropolitan Museum of Art, New York City.
C. W. C. Cunnington, Cecil Willett. *English Women's Clothing in the Nineteenth Century.* London: Faber & Faber, 1937.
Gesz. Geszler, J. *Les Modes du XIXe siècle.* Paris: Ollendorff, 189?.
Goetz (1) Goetz, Walter. *Das Mittelalter bis zum Ausgang der Staufer, 400-1250.* Berlin: Im Propylden-Verlag, 1932.
Goetz (2) ——. *Das Zeitalter der Gotik und Renaissance, 1250-1500.* Berlin: Im Propylden-Verlag, 1932.
Gosse Gosse, A. Bothwell. *The Civilization of the Ancient Egyptians.* London: Jack, 1915; New York: Stokes, 1916.
Heuzey Heuzey, Léon A. *Histoire du costume dans l'antiquité classique.* Paris: Les Belles Lettres, 1935.
Hope Hope, Thomas. *Costume of the Ancients.* London: Bohn, 1841; 2 vols.
Houst. (1) Houston, Mary G., and Hornblower, F. S. *Ancient Egyptian, Assyrian, and Persian Costumes and Decorations.* London: Black, 1920; New York: Macmillan, 1921.
Houst. (2) ——. *Ancient Greek, Roman, and Byzantine Costume and Decoration.* London: Block; New York: Macmillan, 1931.
Klass. *Klassiker der Kunst in Gesamtausgaben.* Stuttgart and Leipzig: Deutsche Verlags-Anstalt, 1904——; 38 vols.
L. Leloir, Maurice. *Histoire du costume de l'antiquité à 1914.* Paris: Ernst, 1933-38; 11 vols.
Met. M. Metropolitan Museum of Art, New York City.
Met. M. L. Metropolitan Museum of Art Library.
Met. M. Pr. Metropolitan Museum of Art Department of Prints
N.Y. P. L. New York (City) Public Library, Room 313.
ph. Photograph(s).
Rac. Racinet, Albert C. A. *Le Costume historique.* Paris: Firmin-Didot, 1876-88; 6 vols.
Ref. Coll. Reference Collection of Photographs of the Metropolitan Museum of Art, New York City.
Rupp. Ruppert, Jacques. *Le Costume.* Paris: Ducher, 1930-31.
Sit. (1) Sitwell, Sacheverell. *Conversation Pieces.* London: Batsford; New York: Scribner's, 1937
Sit. (2) ——. *Narrative Pictures.* London: Batsford; New York: Scribner's, 1938.
vBn. von Boehn, Max. *Das Beiwerk der Mode.* Munich: Bruckman, 1928.

(a), (b), (c), etc., *refer to horizontal rows of pictures*
I, II, III, etc., *refer to position in the row*

Page
frontis. Ph. from the artist's collection.
   vii. After Holbein, in Klass.
   1. After Greek statue in Delphi Museum.
   3. Gosse.
   5. (a) I, II, and III, Rac.
       (b) I, Houst.; II and III, Heuzey.
       (c) I and II, Heuzey; III and IV, Rac.
   6. (a) I, Heuzey; II and III, from *Textiles and Costumes among the Peoples of the*

Page
       Ancient Near East (H. F. Lutz).
       (b) I and III, Heuzey; II, from book cited in (a).
       (c) I, II, III, and IV, Heuzey.
   7. (a) I, II, III, and IV, Rac.
       (b) I and III, Gosse; II, Rac.
       (c) I, II, and III, Gosse.
       (d) I, II, and IV, Gosse; III, Rac.
   8. (a) I and III, Houst. (1); II, Rac.

Page

after Fullmaurer, in N. Y. P. L.; iv, after Sanchez Coello, in N. Y. P. L.

55. After anonymous artist, in National Gallery, London.

56. (a) i, after Moroni, in N. Y. P. L.; ii, after Cranach, in Met. M. L.; iii, after monumental effigy, in N. Y. P. L.

(b) i, after Moroni, in N. Y. P. L.; ii, after Moro, in N. Y. P. L.; iii, after Boissard, in Met. M. Pr.

(c) i, ii, and iv, after Moroni, in N. Y. P. L.; iii, vBn.

57. (a) i, after Moroni; ii and iii, after Moro; all in N. Y. P. L.

(b) i, after J. Amman; ii, after C. Ketel; iii, after Moro; all in N. Y. P. L.

(c) i, after J. Wierix; ii and iii, after Moroni; iv, after F. Clouet; all in N. Y. P. L.

58. (a) i and ii, after Moro; iii and iv, after Moroni; all in N. Y. P. L.

(b) i, ii, and iii, after Moro, in N. Y. P. L.

(c) i, after Cranach; ii and iii, after Moro; all in N. Y. P. L.

(d) i and ii, after Moro; iii, after Titian; all in N. Y. P. L.

59. (a) i, after Zuccaro; ii, L.; iii, after Marcus Gheeraerts; all in N. Y. P. L.

(b) i, after Pretersz; ii, after portrait in National Gallery, London; iii, after Hardwick portrait by unknown artist; all in N. Y. P. L.

(c) i, after Pourbus; ii, iii, and iv, after Zuccaro; all in N. Y. P. L.

60. Entire plate, after N. Hilliard, in N. Y. P. L.

61. (a) i, ii, and iii, after R. Boissard, in Met. M. Pr.

(b) i and iii, after Boissard, in Met. M. Pr.; ii, after school of Zuccaro, in N. Y. P. L.

(c) i, L.; ii and iv, after Goltzius in Met. M. Pr.; iii, vBn.

62. (a) i and iii, after Zuccaro; ii, after school of Clouet; all in N. Y. P. L.

(b) i and iii, in N. Y. P. L.; ii, after W. Rogers, in Met. M. Pr.

(c) i and iv, after Pourbus; ii and iii, after Zuccaro; all in N. Y. P. L.

64. After W. Hollar, in Met. M. Pr.

65. After Rubens, in Klass.

70. (a) i, ii, iii, and iv, L.

(b) i, ii, and iii, Rupp.

(c) i and iii, in N. Y. P. L.; ii, after Rubens, from Klass.

(d) All from L.

Page

71. (a) i, after Merian, in Met. M. Pr.; ii, L.; iii, after English effigy, in Met. M. L.

(b) i, after Van de Pass, in Met. M. Pr.; ii and iii, after Marcus Gheeraerts, in N. Y. P. L.

(c) i, after P. Isaacs, in N. Y. P. L.; ii and iv, after Van de Pass, in Met. M. Pr.; iii, after Goltzius, in Met. M. Pr.

72. (a) i, in Met. M. L.; ii and iii, after Van de Velde, in Met. M. Pr.

(b) i, ii, and iii, after Van Scheyndel, in Met. M. L.

(c) i, ii, iii, and iv, after Van de Velde, in Met. M. Pr.

73. (a) i and iii, L.; ii, after P. Codde, in Met. M. L.; iv, after Rubens, from Klass.

(b) i, L.; ii and iii, after Rubens, from Klass.

(c) i, ii, and iii, after P. van Somer, in N. Y. P. L.

(d) All from L.

74. (a) i, L.; ii, after a painting at Petworth, England, in N. Y. P. L.; iii, after W. Akersloot, in N. Y. P. L.

(b) i, after Van Dyck, from Klass.; ii, in N. Y. P. L.; iii, after J. de Saint-Ingy, in Met. M. Pr.

(c) i, after J. de Saint-Ingy, in Met. M. L.; ii and iii, in Met. M. L.; iv, after Van Dyck, from Klass.

75. Entire plate after Van Dyck, from Klass.

76. (a) i, after Savery; ii, after Callot; iii, after A. Bosse; all in Met. M. Pr.

(b) i, after Rubens, from Klass.; ii, after Maes, in Ref. Coll.; iii, in Ref. Coll.

(c) All in Met. M. Pr.

77. (a) i, ii, and iii, after A. Bosse, in Met. M. Pr.

(b) i, after A. Bosse, in Met. M. Pr.; ii and iii, after Rembrandt, from Klass.

(c) i and ii, after A. Bosse, in Met. M. Pr.; iii, after Van Dyck, from Klass.; iv, in Ref. Coll.

78. (a) i, ii, iii, and iv, after A. Bosse, in Met. M. Pr.

(b) i, L.; ii, iii, and iv, after A. Bosse, in Met. M. Pr.; v, after Van Dyck, from Klass.

(c) After LeNain, in N. Y. P. L.

(d) i, L.; ii, after J. Steen, in Ref. Coll.; others, L.

79. After Velázquez, in Klass.

80. (a) i, after Pourbus, in Ref. Coll.; ii, after French print, in Met. M. Pr.; iii, after W. Hollar, in Met. M. Pr.

Page

(b) I, after A. Bosse, in Met. M. Pr.; II, after Van Dyck, from Klass.; III, after Terborch, in Ref. Coll.

(c) I, L.; II, after Van der Helst, in Met. M. Pr.; III, after Goesbeck, in Met. M. L.; IV, after Van Dyck, in Met. M. L.

81. Entire plate after W. Hollar, in Met. M. Pr.

82. (a) I, L.; II, after von Sandrart; III and IV, after W. Hollar, in Met. M. Pr.

(b) and (c), after Hollar, in Met. M. Pr.

(d) Shoes at left, L.; muff and patten, after Hollar, in Met. M. Pr.; shoe at right, after Van Dyck, from Klass.

83. (a) I, II, III, and IV, L.

(b) I, after Terborch, in Ref. Coll.

(c) I, L.; II, III, IV, and V, after W. Hollar, in Met. M. Pr.

(d) I and III, after Hollar, in Met. M. Pr.; II, after H. Beaubrun; IV, L.

(e) Child, after J. Steen, in Ref. Coll.; others, L.

84. (a) I and II, after de Hooch; III, after Vermeer; all in Ref. Coll.

(b) I, in Met. M. Pr.; II, after Hals, in Ref. Coll.; III, after Terborch, in Ref. Coll.

(c) I, II, and IV, L.; III, after de Hooch, in Ref. Coll.

85. After "Fête Book," in Met. M. Pr.

86. (a) I and II, Rupp.; III and IV, after J. Steen, in Ref. Coll.

(b) After J. Steen, in Ref. Coll.

(c) I, L.; II, after W. Hollar, in Met. M. Pr.; III, after J. Steen, in Ref. Coll.; IV, vBn.

(d) L.

(e) I and II, in Met. M. L.; III, L.; IV, after Terborch, in Ref. Coll.

(f) Upper low shoe, after J. Steen, in Ref. Coll.; lower shoe and boot, after Terborch, in Ref. Coll.; others, L.

87. (a) I, II, and III, L.

(b) I, after Netscher, in N. Y. P. L.; II, Rupp.; III, after Van der Temple.

(c) I and III, after C. Le Brun; II, after de Saint Jean; IV, after R. de Hooghe; all in Met. M. Pr.

88. (a) I and III, after de Hooch, in Ref. Coll.; II, L.

(b) I and II, after de Hooch; III, after Terborch; all in Ref. Coll.

(c) I, II, III, and IV, after de Hooch, in Ref. Coll.

89. (a) I, II, and III, L.; IV, Rupp.

(b) I, after de Saint Jean, in Met. M. Pr.; II, L.; III, vBn.

Page

(c) I, after painting by Abbess de Maubuisson, in Met. M. L.; II, after de Hooch, in N. Y. P. L.; III, after de Saint Jean, in N. Y. P. L.

(d) All from L.

90. (a) I, L.; II, after Lepautre, in Met. M. Pr.; III, after S. Leclerk, in Met. M. Pr.

(b) I and III, French fashion plates in Met. M. Pr.; II, after Van der Neer, Met. M. L.

(c) I, II, III, and IV, after D. Loggan, in Met. M. L.

91. (a) I, after N. Bonnart, in Met. M. Pr.; II, after effigy, Trinity Almshouses, London, in Met. M. Pr.; III, after Vatek, in Met. M. Pr.

(b) I, II, and III, after Bonnart, in Met. M. Pr.

(c) I, II, and III, after Bonnart, in Met. M. Pr.; IV, after J. Weenix, in Met. M. L.

92. (a) I, vBn.; II and III, in Met. M. L.; IV, after N. Bonnart, in Met. M. Pr.

(b) I, after N. Arnoult, in Met. M. Pr.; II and III, L.

(c) I, II, and III, L.

(d) I, II, and III, after Arnoult, in Met. M. Pr.; IV, after J. Steen, in Ref. Coll.; V and VI, L.

93. (a) I, II, and III, after French fashion plates, in Met. M. Pr.

(b) I and III, after French fashion plates, in Met. M. Pr.; II, after Berey, from L.

(c) I and III, L.; II and IV, after N. Bonnart, in Met. M. Pr.

94. (a) I, II, III, and IV, after N. Bonnart, in Met. M. Pr.

(b) I, II, and III, after French fashion plates, in Met. M. Pr.

(c) and (d) All from L.

96. After Debucourt, in Met. M. Pr.

97. After Watteau, from Klass.

102. (a) I, after E. Picart; II, after N. Arnoult; III, after Guérard; all in Met. M. Pr.

(b) I, L.; II, after Largillière, in Met. M. L.; III, in Met. M. Pr.

(c) I, II, III, and IV, after E. Picart, in Met. M. Pr.

103. (a) and (b), after Picart, in Met. M. L.

(c) I and II, L.; III, in Met. M. L.

(d) All from L.

104. (a) I, II, and III, after Watteau, in Met. M. Pr.

(b) I and III, after Watteau, from Klass.; II, after unknown artist, in National Gallery, London.

Page

(c) I, after unknown artist, in National Gallery, London; II, after Watteau, from Klass.; III, after Tournières, in Met. M. L.; IV, L.

105. (a) I, L.; II, after Watteau, from Klass.; III and IV, after E. Picart, in Met. M. Pr.

(b) and (c), after Watteau, from Klass.

(d) I and II, after de Troy, in Met. M. L.; III, L.; IV, after Watteau, from Klass.; V, after Picart, in Met. M. Pr.

106. (a) I, after A. Hérisset, in Met. M. Pr.; II, after C. Troost, in N. Y. P. L.; III, after C. Troost, in Met. M. L.

(b) I, after Watteau, from Klass.; II, L.; III, in Met. M. Pr.

(c) I, in Met. M. Pr.; II, after unknown artist, in National Gallery, London; III and IV, after Justacorps, in Met. M. Pr.

107. (a) I, II, III, and IV, L.

(b) I, after Lancret, in Met. M. L.; II, vBn.; III, after Gravelot, in Met. M. L.

(c) I and III, after Chardin, in Met. M. L.; II, in Met. M. L.

(d) All from L.

108. (a) I, after Chardin; II, after Dumont; III, after Hogarth; all in Met. M. L.

(b) I, after Hogarth; II, after G. Hamilton; III, after de Troy; all in Met. M. L.

(c) I, II, and III, after Rigaud; IV, after Gravelot; all in Met. M. Pr.

109. After Hogarth, in Met. M. Pr.

110. (a) I and III, after Chardin; II, after Longhi; all in Met. M. L.

(b) I, after J. E. Nilson; II, after Hogarth; III, after J. Wills; all in Met. M. L.

(c) I, after Chardin; II, after Liotard, III, after Boydell; IV, after Moreau, "Trois suites d'estampes"; all in Met. M. L.

111. Entire plate after Hogarth, in Met. M. L.

112. (a) I, after Saint-Aubin, in Met. M. L.; II and III, after Hogarth, in Met. M. L.; IV, Rupp.

(b) I, after Lancret; II, after Gainsborough; III, after Chardin; all in Met. M. L.

(c) I, II, and IV, after Gainsborough; III, after Hogarth; all in Met. M. L.

(d) All from L.

113. (a) I, after Boucher, in Ref. Coll.; II, group after Gainsborough, in Met. M. L.

(b) I and III, after Gainsborough, in Met. M. L.; II, in Met. M. L.

(c) I, II, III, and IV, after E. Bouchardon, in Met. M. Pr.

Page

114. (a) I, L.; II and III, after Longhi, in Met. M. L.; IV, vBn.

(b) I, after Van Loo; II, after Boucher; III, after Longhi; all in Met. M. L.

(c) I, after Hogarth, in Met. M. L.; II, vBn.; III, after Nattier, in Met. M. L.

(d) Gloves, L.; figures after Gainsborough, in Met. M. L.

115. After Rowlandson, in Met. M. L.

117. (a) I, after Batoni; II and III, after N. Dance, from Sit. (1)

(b) I and IV, after Zoffany; II and III, after A. Devis; all from Sit. (1)

(c) All after Stubbs, from Sit. (1)

118. (a) I, after Cochin, in Met. M. L.; II, III, and IV, vBn.

(b) I, after Cochin; II, after Boucher; III, after Bradel; all in Met. M. L.

(c) I, II, and III, L.

(d) All from L.

119. (a) I and III, after Chodowiecki, in Met. M. Pr.; III, after Moreau, in Met. M. Pr.

(b) I, after Zoffany, from Sit. (1); II, after Drouais, in Met. M. L.; III, after F. Cotes, in Met. M. L.

(c) I, II, III, and IV, after Moreau, "Trois suites d'estampes," in Met. M. L.

120. (a) I, after Walton, from Sit. (2); II, after Moreau, "Trois suites d'estampes," in Met. M. L.; III, after J. Collet, from Sit. (1)

(b) and (c), after Moreau, "Trois suites d'estampes," in Met. M. L.

121. (a) I, after Tischbein, in Met. M. L.; II and III, after Chodowiecki, from vBn.; IV, L.

(b) I and III, vBn.; II, after Saint-Aubin, in Met. M. L.

(c) I, II, and III, vBn.

(d) All from L.

122. (a) I, after Moreau, "Trois suites d'estampes," in Met. M. L.; II, after J. R. Smith, in Met. M. L.; III, after Debucourt, in Met. M. Pr.; IV, after J. Hickel, in Met. M. L.

(b) I, after Vigée-Lebrun, in Ref. Coll.; II, after Roslin, in Met. M. L.; III, in C. Inst.

(c) I, after Vigée-Lebrun, in Ref. Coll.; II, after Hoppner, in Met. M. L.; III, after Debucourt, in Met. M. Pr.

(d) Hoops, vBn.; others, after G. Stubbs, in Met. M. L.

123. (a) I and III, after R. Dighton, from Sit. (2); II, after Zoffany, from Sit. (1)

Page

(b) I, after Gainsborough, in Met. M. L.; II, after Zoffany, from Sit. (1); III, vBn.

(c) I and IV, after Zoffany, from Sit. (1); II, after W. Williams, from Sit. (2); III, after Gainsborough, in Met. M. L.

124. (a) I, II, and III, after Debucourt, in Met. M. Pr.; IV, vBn.

(b) I, after Debucourt; II, after Danloux; III, after Girodet; all in Met. M. Pr.

(c) I and II, after Debucourt, in Met. M. Pr.; III, after David, in Met. M. L.

(d) I, II, III, and IV, after David, in Met. M. L.

125. Entire plate after Debucourt, in Met. M. Pr.
126. Entire plate after Goya, in Met. M. L.
128. Ph. from the George Eastman House Collection, Rochester, N. Y.
129. After Ingres, in Met. M. L.
134. (a) I, II, and III, after Ingres, in Met. M. L.

(b) I, after Ingres, in Met. M. L.; II, Gesz.; III, vBn.

(c) I, vBn.; II and IV, after B. Marshall, in Met. M. L.; III, in C. Inst.

135. (a) I and II, after Ingres, in Met. M. L.; III and IV, in C. Inst.

(b) and (c), central figure, after David, in Met. M. L.; others, in C. Inst.

(d) Spencer, Rupp.; others, C. W. C.

136. (a) I and III, Gesz.; II, in C. Inst.

(b) I, II, and III, Gesz.

(c) I, II, III, and IV, after Debucourt, in Met. M. Pr.

137. (a) I and II, after David; III and IV, after Ingres; all in Met. M. L.

(b) I and II, after David, in Met. M. L.; III, vBn.

(c) I, II, and III, after David, in Met. M. L.

(d) All from C. W. C.

138. (a) and (b), Gesz.

(c) I, III, and IV, after Mésangère, from vBn.; II, after B. Marshall, in Met. M. L.

139. (a) I, II, and III, vBn.

(b) I, after Ingres, in Met. M. L.; II, from *Life in Regency and Early Victorian Times* (E. B. Chancellor); III, Rupp.

(c) I, after Dighton, from book cited in (b); II, after Partridge, from Sit. (1); III, Rupp.; IV, after J. Ferneley, from book cited in (6).

140. (a) I, II, III, and IV, C. W. C.

(b) I, after Hessan; II, in C. Inst.; III, after Ingres, in Met. M. L.

(c) In C. Inst.

(d) C. W. C.

Page

141. (a) I, II, and III, Gesz.

(b) I and II, Gesz.; III, after Ingres, in Met. M. L.

(c) I, II, III, and IV, Gesz.

142. (a) I, after Grévedon, from vBn.; II, after Deveria, from vBn.; III and IV, vBn.

(b) I, in C. Inst.; II and III, after Ingres, in Met. M. L.

(c) I, II, and III, after Ingres, in Met. M. L.

(d) All from C. W. C.

143. (a) I, vBn.; II, from *Life in Regency and Early Victorian Times* (E. B. Chancellor); III, Gesz.

(b) I and II, in C. Inst.; III, vBn.

(c) I, after Tschernezow, from vBn.; II, vBn.; III, Rupp.

144. After Guys, in Met. M. L.

145. (a) I and III, Sit. (2); II, vBn.

(b) I, II, and III, after Winterhalter, from vBn.

(c) I, after Bertall; II, III, and IV, after Gavarni, from vBn.

146. (a) I and II, in C. Inst.; III, vBn.; IV, ph. by D. O. Hill, in Met. M. Pr.

(b) I, vBn.; II, after Chalon, from vBn.; III, after Ingres, in Met. M. L.

(c) In C. Inst.

(d) C. W. C.

147. Entire plate, ph. from the George Eastman House Collection, Rochester, N. Y.

148. (a) I, after Dyce, from Sit. (2); II, ph. from vBn.; III, from *American Monitor of Fashion* (magazine), 1854.

(b) I, II, and III, ph. from vBn.

(c) I, II, III, and IV, fashion plates in C. Inst.

149. (a) I, II, and III, ph. from *Histoire de la photographie* (R. Lecuyer).

(b) and (c), ph. from the George Eastman House Collection, Rochester, N. Y.

150. (a) I, II, and III, C. W. C.; IV, in C. Inst.

(b) I, vBn.; II, after Courbet, in Met. M. L.; III, after W. M. Egley, from vBn.

(c) I, II, and III, after Ingres, in Met. M. L.

(d) I and III, C. W. C.; II, after Ingres, in Met. M. L.

151. (a) I, II, and III, ph. by Antoine, in Met. M. Pr.

(b) I and II, ph. by Antoine; III, ph. by Braun; all in Met. M. Pr.

(c) I, II, III, and IV, ph. by Antoine, in Met. M. Pr.

152. (a) I, II, and III, ph. by Disderi, from the George Eastman House Collection, Rochester, N. Y.

Page

(b) and (c), ph. from the George Eastman House Collection.

153. (a) Ph. from the George Eastman House Collection, Rochester, N. Y.

(b) I, ph. by D. O. Hill, in Met. M. Pr.; II, ph. by Braun, in Met. M. Pr.; III, ph. from vBn.

(c) Ph. from the artist's collection.

154. Ph. by Braun, in Met. M. Pr.

156. (a) I and II, ph. from vBn.; III, ph. by Brady, from *Mr. Lincoln's Camera Man, Mathew B. Brady* (R. Meredith).

(b) I and III, after Monet; II, after Manet; all in Met. M. L.

(c) Ph. from the artist's collection.

157. (a) I and II, C. W. C.; III, in C. Inst.; IV, vBn.

(b) I, II, and III, vBn.

(c) I and II, vBn.; III, in C. Inst.

(d) All from C. W. C.

158. Entire plate, ph. by Lewis Carroll, in Princeton University Library.

159. (a) I, II, and III, vBn.

(b) I, vBn.; II and III, ph. from the artist's collection.

(c) I, II, III, and IV, in C. Inst.

160. (a) I and II, ph. from the artist's collection; III, ph. from the George Eastman House Collection, Rochester, N. Y.

(b) Ph. from the George Eastman House Collection.

(c) I, III, and IV, ph. in C. Inst.; II, ph. by Lewis Carroll, in Princeton University Library.

161. (a) I, II, and III, C. W. C.

(b) I, after Tissot, from Sit. (2); II, after Manet, in Met. M. L.; III, after Renoir, in Met. M. L.

(c) I, II, III, and IV, in C. Inst.

162. (a) I and II, after Manet, in Met. M. L.; III and IV, C. W. C.

(b) I and II, ph. from the artist's collection; III, in C. Inst.

(c) I, II, and III, after Manet, in Met. M. L.

(d) Ph. from the artist's collection.

Page

163. (a) I, ph. from the artist's collection; II and III, vBn.

(b) I, C. W. C.; II, ph. from the George Eastman House Collection, Rochester, N. Y.; III, ph. from unknown source.

(c) I and II, in C. Inst.; III, vBn.; IV, after Renoir, in Met. M. L.

164. (a) I, II, and III, vBn.

(b) and (c), in C. Inst.

165. (a) I and II, in C. Inst.; III, vBn.; IV, after Manet, in Met. M. L.

(b) I, II, and III, after Manet, in Met. M. L.

(c) I, vBn.; II and III, after Manet, in Met. M. L.

(d) All from C. W. C.

166. (a) I, II, and IV, ph. from C. W. C.; III, after Manet, in Met. M. L.

(b) From contemporary fashion plates.

(c) I, ph. from C. W. C.; II and III, ph. in C. Inst.; IV, ph. from *Music Hall Parade* (M. W. Disher).

168. Ph. from the artist's collection.

169. Ph. from the artist's collection.

172. (a) I, II, III, and IV, in C. Inst.

(b) I, II, and III, in C. Inst.

(c) In C. Inst.

(d) I, in C. Inst.; others, C. W. C.

173. Entire plate after Toulouse-Lautrec, in Met. M. L.

174. (a) I, ph. from the artist's collection; II and III, ph. from *Vogue* (magazine).

(b) I, vBn.; II and III, ph. from *Vogue*.

(c) I, II, III, and IV, in C. Inst.

175. All ph.:

(a) I, II, and III, from *Vogue* (magazine).

(b) From *The Twentieth Century Home Encyclopedia and Gazetteer*.

(c) I, from *Vogue*; II, III, and IV, vBn.

176. All ph.:

(a) I and II, from *Vogue* (magazine); III, from the artist's collection.

(b) From *Vogue*.

(c) I, II, and III, from *Vogue*; IV, vBn.

177. Entire plate, ph. from *Vogue* (magazine).

Sources for "American Costume"

KEY

Beebe	Beebe, Lucius M., and Clegg, Charles. *U. S. West, the Saga of Wells Fargo*. New York: Dutton, 1949.
C. Inst.	Costume Institute of the Metropolitan Museum of Art, New York City.
Jack.	Jackson, Clarence S. *Picture Maker of the Old West, William H. Jackson*. New York: Scribner's, 1947
Lib. Cong.	Collection of Prints and Photographs of the Library of Congress, Washington, D. C.
M.C.N.Y.	Museum of the City of New York.
Mered.	Meredith, Roy. *Mr. Lincoln's Camera Man, Mathew B. Brady*. New York: Scribner's, 1946.
N.Y.H.S.	New York Historical Society, New York City.
N.Y.P.L.	New York (City) Public Library, Room 300.
ph.	Photograph(s).
P. Phot.	*Philadelphia Photographer* (later, *Photographic Journal of America*).
Rogers	Rogers, Agnes. *Women Are Here To Stay*. New York: Harper, 1949.
S&H	Collection of photographs by Southworth and Hawes, in Metropolitan Museum of Art (N.Y.C.), Department of Prints.
Schmitt	Schmitt, Martin F., and Brown, Dee. *Fighting Indians of the West*. New York: Scribner's, 1948.

(a), (b), (c), etc., *refer to horizontal rows of pictures*
I, II, III, etc., *refer to position in the row*

Page
179. Ph. from the artist's collection.
181. Ph. from the Frederick H. Meserve Collection in New York City.
184. (a) I, from *Photography and the American Scene* (R. Taft); II and III, Beebe; IV, S&H.
    (b) I, II, and III, S&H.
    (c) I, II, III, and IV, Mered.
185. All ph.:
    (a) I and III, S&H; II, from *Photography and the American Scene* (R. Taft).
    (b) I, II, and III, S&H.
    (c) I, II, and IV, from book cited in (a); III, in N. Y. H. S.
186. Entire plate from *Lincoln, His Life in Photographs* (S. Lorant).
187. (a) and (b), in N. Y. H. S.
    (c) I, II, and III, from *The American Past* (R. P. Butterfield); IV, P. Phot.
188. All ph.:
    (a) I, II, and III, from *Lincoln, His Life in Photographs* (S. Lorant).
    (b) I, from book cited in (a); II, III, and IV, Jack.

Page
    (c) I, II, and III, in M. C. N. Y.; IV, from book cited in (a).
189. All ph.:
    (a) I, from *Lincoln, His Life in Photographs* (S. Lorant); II, Jack.; III, Mered.
    (b) and (c), Mered.
190. All ph.:
    (a) I and III, P. Phot.; II, in N. Y. H. S.
    (b) I, II, and III, in N. Y. H. S.
    (c) I, II, III, and IV, in C. Inst.
191. All ph.:
    (a) I, from *The American Past* (R. P. Butterfield); II and III, in N. Y. H. S.
    (b) All from the collection of Wesley M. Angle, Rochester, N. Y.
    (c) I and II, in C. Inst.; III, P. Phot.; IV, from the George Eastman House Collection, Rochester, N. Y.
192. All ph.:
    (a) I, II, and III, in N. Y. P. L.
    (b) I and II, P. Phot.; III, in M. C. N. Y.
    (c) I, P. Phot.; II and III, from *The American Past* (R. P. Butterfield); IV, in M. C. N. Y.

Page

195. Entire plate, ph. from the collection of Mrs. Pauline Dakin Taft, Oberlin, Ohio.

196. Entire plate, ph. from the collection of Mrs. Pauline Dakin Taft, Oberlin, Ohio.

197. All ph.:
(a) I, P. Phot.; II, in Lib. Cong.; III, Rogers.
(b) I, II, and III, in M. C. N. Y.
(c) I, from the George Eastman House Collection, Rochester, N. Y.; II, III, and IV, from the collection of Mrs. Pauline Dakin Taft, Oberlin, Ohio.

198. (a) and (b), after Eakins, from *Thomas Eakins, His Life and Work* (L. Goodrich).
(c) I, II, and III, after Eakins; IV, ph.; all from book cited in (a).

199. All ph.:
(a) and (b), from the Byron Collection, in M. C. N. Y.
(c) I, II, III, and IV, by E. A. Austin, in M. C. N. Y.

200. Entire plate, ph. from the Byron Collection, in M. C. N. Y.

201. (a) I and II, ph. from *The Book of Sport* (W. Patten, ed.); III, ph. in C. Inst.
(b) I, ph. from Rogers; II, ph. from the Alexander Alland Collection, North Salem, N. Y.; III, after Sargent, from Metropolitan Museum (N.Y.C.) collection.
(c) I, II, and IV, ph. in N. Y. P. L.; III, ph. from book cited in (a).

202. All ph.:
(a) and (b), from the Byron Collection, in M. C. N. Y.
(c) I and II, from the artist's collection; III, from *Our Times* (M. Sullivan).

204. Ph. from the artist's collection.

205. Ph. from the Levi Strauss Collection in San Francisco, Calif.

207. (a) I, from *Across the Wide Missouri* (B. De Voto); II, in N. Y. P. L.; III, after Remington, from *Frederic Remington, Artist of the Old West* (H. McCracken).
(b) I and II, ph. from *Kit Carson Days* (E. L. Sabin); III, after Remington, from *Frederic Remington*.
(c) I and II, from *Across the Wide Missouri;* III, ph. from *The River of the West* (F. F. Victor); IV, ph. from *Kit Carson Days*.

208. All ph.:
(a) I and II, Jack.; III, from *Gold Rush Album* (J. H. Jackson).

Page

(b) I and III, Beebe; II, by Brady, in N. Y. H. S.
(c) I, from *Hudson's Bay Company Series;* II, in N. Y. P. L.; III, Mered.; IV, by Brady, in N. Y. H. S.

209. All ph.:
(a) I, II, III, and IV, Schmitt.
(b) I, II, and III, Beebe.
(c) I, from *Memoirs* (M. A. Maverick); II and III, from *From the Gold Mine to the Pulpit* (T. L. James); IV, from *Trails of Yesterday* (J. Bratt).

210. All ph.:
(a) I, II, and III, from *The Overland Stage to California* (F. A. Root and W. E. Connelley).
(b) I, in N. Y. P. L.; II, from book cited in (a); III, from *Early Western Photographs, 1862-1897* (Union Pacific Historical Museum), in N. Y. P. L.
(c) I, from book cited in (a); II, Schmitt; III and IV, from *Broncho Charlie* (G. S. Erskine).

211. Entire plate, ph. from the George Eastman House Collection, Rochester, N. Y.

212. All ph.:
(a) I, II, and III, Schmitt.
(b) and (c), Jack.

213. Ph. by S. D. Butcher.

216. All ph.:
(a) I, from *Jeff Milton* (J. E. Haley); II, from *Triggernometry* (E. Cunningham); III, in N. Y. P. L.
(b) I and III, from *Triggernometry;* II, Beebe.
(c) I and IV, Beebe; II, by Grabill, in Lib. Cong.; III, in N. Y. P. L.

217. All ph.:
(a) I, II, and III, Jack.
(b) and (c), Schmitt.

218. All ph.:
(a) I, from *Black Hills Trails* (J. Brown and A. M. Willard); II, Jack.
(b) I, Schmitt; II, from *Triggernometry* (E. Cunningham); III, in N. Y. P. L.
(c) I, from *The Overland Stage to California* (F. A. Root and W. E. Connelley); II and III, in N. Y. P. L.; IV, from *We Pointed Them North* (E. C. Abbott).

219. All ph.:
(a) I and II, Schmitt.
(b) I and II, Jack.; III, in N. Y. P. L.
(c) I, II, III, and IV, Schmitt.

220. Entire plate, ph. by Butcher, in Lib. Cong.

Page

221. Entire plate, ph. in Lib. Cong.
222. Entire plate, ph. by J. S. Baker, in Lib. Cong.
223. Entire plate, ph. in Lib. Cong.
224. All ph.:
    (a) I, from *Life;* II, in N. Y. P. L.; III, from *The XIT Ranch of Texas* (J. E. Haley).
    (b) I, in N. Y. P. L.; II, Beebe; III, from book cited in (a).
    (c) I, by Grabill, in Lib. Cong.; II, from *The Overland Stage to California* (F. A. Root and W. E. Connelley); III and IV, from *Triggernometry* (E. Cunningham).
225. Entire plate, ph. in Lib. Cong.
226. All ph.:
    (a) and (b), in Lib. Cong.
    (c) I, from the artist's collection; II and III, from *Pioneer History of Custer County* (S. D. Butcher); IV, in N. Y. P. L.
228. Ph. from the artist's collection.
229. Ph. by S. D. Butcher.
231. (a) I and III, ph. in N. Y. P. L.; II, after Remington, from *Frederic Remington, Artist of the Old West* (H. McCracken).
    (b) I, ph. from *Hands Up!* (F. E. Sutton); II, ph. from *The Trail Drivers of Texas* (J. M. Hunter); III, ph. from *Fifty Years on the Old Frontier* (J. H. Cook).
    (c) I, ph. from *We Pointed Them North* (E. C. Abbott); II, ph. from *Panhandle-Plains Historical Review,* 1944; III and IV, ph. from *Charles M. Russell, the Cowboy Artist* (R. F. Adams and H. E. Britzman).
232. All ph.:
    (a) I, from *Banbrytaren* (S. J. Kronberg); II, from *Tales from Buffalo Land* (U. L. Burdick); III, from *Panhandle-Plains Historical Review,* 1944.
    (b) I, from *Broncho Charlie* (G. S. Erskine); II and IV, from *Charles M. Russell, the Cowboy Artist* (R. F. Adams and H. E. Britzman); III and V, from *Wyoming Cowboy Days* (C. A. Guernsey).
    (c) I, III, and IV, in N. Y. P. L.; II, from *We Pointed Them North* (E. C. Abbott).
233. All ph.:
    (a) I, from *Frontier Trails* (F. M. Canton); II, in Lib. Cong.; III, from *Kaleidoscopic Lives* (J. H. Taylor).

Page

    (b) I and II, in N. Y. P. L.; III, from *Pardner of the Wind* (N. H. Thorp and N. M. Clark).
    (c) I and II, in N. Y. P. L.; III, from *Riata and Spurs* (C. A. Siringo); IV, from *History of the Oregon Country* (H. W. Scott).
234. All ph.:
    (a) I and II, from the artist's collection; III, courtesy of Struthers Burt, Jackson Hole, Wyoming.
    (b) I, II, and III, by E. Smith, from *The XIT Ranch of Texas* (J. E. Haley).
    (c) I, II, and III, from book cited in (b); IV, from *Desperate Men* (J. D. Horan).
235. All ph.:
    (a) I, II, and III, in Lib. Cong.
    (b) I, in N. Y. P. L.; II, from *Jeff Milton* (J. E. Haley); III, from *Panhandle-Plains Historical Review,* 1944.
    (c) I, II, III, and IV, in N. Y. P. L.
236. Entire plate, ph. in N. Y. P. L.
237. All ph.:
    (a) I, from *Texas Cowboys* (D. Coolidge); II, III, and IV, from *Old California Cowboys* (D. Coolidge).
    (b) I and III, from *Charles M. Russell, the Cowboy Artist* (R. F. Adams and H. E. Britzman); II, in N. Y. P. L.
    (c) I, from *Life;* II and IV, from book cited in (b); III, from *Panhandle-Plains Historical Review,* 1944.
238. All ph.:
    (a) and (c), from *The Cowboy* (P. A. Rollins).
    (b) I, II, and III, from the artist's collection.
240. Ph. from the artist's collection.
241. Ph. from Rogers.
244. (a) I, II, and III, ph. in C. Inst.
    (b) All ph. in M. C. N. Y.
    (c) I, ph. from *Vogue* (magazine); II, after Paxton, from Rogers; III, ph. from Rogers; IV, ph. in C. Inst.
245. All ph.:
    (a) and (b), in M. C. N. Y.
    (c) I and II, in M. C. N. Y.; III and IV, from the Byron Collection, in M. C. N. Y.
246. Entire plate, ph. from *Vogue* (magazine).
247. Entire plate, ph. from *Vogue* (magazine).
248. All ph.:
    (a) I, II, III, and IV, from *Vogue* (magazine).
    (b) I, II, and III, Rogers.
    (c) I, II, III, and IV, from *Vogue.*